JAGUAR XJ SERIES SALOONS

MARK SUTHERLAND

Foreword by
Quentin Willson

AMBERLEY

First published 2024

Amberley Publishing
The Hill, Stroud,
Gloucestershire, GL5 4EP

www.amberley-books.com

Copyright © Mark Sutherland, 2024

The right of Mark Sutherland to be identified as the Author of this work has been asserted in accordance with the Copyright, Designs and Patents Act 1988.

All rights reserved. No part of this book may be reprinted or reproduced or utilised in any form or by any electronic, mechanical or other means, now known or hereafter invented, including photocopying and recording, or in any information storage or retrieval system, without the permission in writing from the Publishers.

ISBN: 978 1 3981 2149 2 (print)
ISBN: 978 1 3981 2150 8 (ebook)

British Library Cataloguing in Publication Data.
A catalogue record for this book is available from the British Library.

Typeset in 10pt on 13pt Celeste.
Typesetting by SJmagic DESIGN SERVICES, India.
Printed in the UK.

Appointed GPSR EU Representative: Easy Access System Europe Oü, 16879218
Address: Mustamäe tee 50, 10621, Tallinn, Estonia
Contact Details: gpsr.requests@easproject.com, +358 40 500 3575

Contents

Foreword by Quentin Willson	4
Origins: The Story of the World's Oldest XJ	7
Series 1 XJ: 1968–1973	19
Series 2 XJ: 1973–1979	32
XJ-C: 1975–1977	45
Series 3 XJ: 1978–1992	68
At the Heart of Every XJ	79
A Sad Goodbye	89
Bibliography	91
Acknowledgements	94

Foreword by Quentin Willson

I well remember the excitement of those first XJs in 1969. Charlie – a school friend – had been bragging for months that his father had ordered 'one of those new Jags' and when it arrived, he'd promised to pick us up from school. The appointed day arrived, and Charlie's dad pulled up in his spanking-new, white, G registration XJ6 4.2 automatic. I can still see it now. Shiny wood, soft red leather, instruments like a plane. Plush, silent, fast. And that new Jaguar smell. He spent the journey home spouting hyperbole: 'As smooth as a Rolls-Royce', 'The best car in the world', 'Jaguar's finest saloon'. But I knew all this. Because my dad had

Quentin Willson.

a Daimler Sovereign – the older 420 version – and as a car-crazy eleven-year-old I could see and feel the difference. I was so jealous. The XJ was from the future. Dad's Daimler was the past. For every big car owner this was a transformational moment. Everything that had gone before looked old – instantly. A year-long waiting list built up and the normally acerbic *CAR* magazine voted the XJ 'Car of the Year'. Charlie ragged me mercilessly about my dad's 'used Daimler'. In the end I had to thump him.

That childhood trauma must have stayed with me because I went on to own a dozen XJs. Everything from a Regency Red 1970 4.2, through Series 2s, Series 3s, an XJ 40 and a slinky black X350 XJR. My abiding memory is of the comfort, poise, elegance, refinement and speed that were rightly hailed as XJ hallmarks over the model's remarkable fifty-year production. Charlie's dad may have been repeating the stuff the Jaguar salesman had told him, but he was absolutely right. The XJ was, at the time, the most refined saloon money could buy and when the 140-mph V12 arrived in 1972, it was also the world's fastest. In the decades before Mercedes AMG and BMW M, XJs ruled the fast lane. Sir William Lyons' final design changed the genre of the luxury car forever. *Autocar* called the XJ12 'a marvellous achievement, deservedly the envy of the world'.

But it was a miracle that the XJ was built at all. Throughout the 1970s Browns Lane was disrupted by strikes and it wasn't unusual for buyers to collect their new XJs with parts missing that had to be later fitted by dealers. Quality and reliability dived, a global fuel crisis and mergers with BMC, and later British Leyland, sabotaged sales, and it wasn't until the brilliant Pininfarina refresh of the Series 3 in 1979 that the XJ got its mojo back. The XJ story is a triumph of tenacity over resources, spearheaded by visionary Coventry engineers who instinctively knew that serene ride quality, smooth drive trains, sharp steering and sweet engines were exactly what buyers wanted. They also managed to distil that magical Jaguar DNA that became affectionately known as 'Best of British'. Despite quality issues, poor external parts suppliers, ageing factories, industrial unrest, and geopolitical upheavals, the XJ was, for many years, one of the most desirable luxury saloons in the world.

That the Jaguar XJ brand survived and prospered for so long when so many external forces were ranged against it is one of the British motor industry's most surprising success stories. In 1979, after a less-than-perfect 12,000-mile test, *Autocar* magazine said: 'The Coventry-made marvel ... in a car like this the faults hardly matter!' Such flattering indulgence from a respected motoring title gives us an idea of the tremendous goodwill that both Jaguar and the XJ enjoyed in Britain. The growing threat from BMW and Mercedes will have stirred some patriotism, but it's important to understand that the XJ wasn't just admired; it was *loved.* As a symbol of Britishness and a metaphor for our once successful car industry, it held a special place in the nation's heart. In the 1990s Margaret Thatcher's Cabinet pleaded to be driven in XJs rather than Rovers because of their 'comfort and status' and the XJ was the official car for prime ministers up to Boris Johnson. XJs appeared on screen in *Skyfall, Spectre, Die Another Day, The Equaliser, The New Avengers, The Protectors* and *The Sweeney*. And casting a 1981 Sovereign Series 3 as transport for the likeable but raffish George Cole in *Minder* was no accident – the XJ had become a national treasure.

But drive an XJ today – even a Series 1 – and you'll be amazed how poised, smooth and modern it still feels. That special alchemy of soft ride quality, low noise and vibration and quick responses is what made the XJ such a great car. And its long, slippery shape with liquid lines and tapering tail is even more beguiling than it was back in 1969. So, sit back and enjoy this celebration of one of Britain's most admired Jaguars and remember that right now the XJ is still a tantalisingly cheap classic car. A reasonable mileage, factory black Series 3 4.2 with Kent alloys can be yours for less than £10,000. I'd have one in a heartbeat.

Quentin Willson, August 2023

Origins: The Story of the World's Oldest XJ

The Series 1 was such a transformative model for Jaguar, you can see all the pedigree in its lines. It has been fascinating digging out the history of this particular car, which has been made with such care and attention to detail. It's the opposite of a Friday afternoon car! It is such a pleasure to drive, and to help preserve this historic car for the future.
Adrian Massey, owner MWK 28G, pre-production Series 1 XJ6 2.8-litre automatic

Before It Began

In the early 1960s Jaguar Cars had an extensive saloon car offering. The Mark 2, which had started life as the Mark 1 in 1955, was selling well in its new guise, along with the iconic E-Type. In some cases, there were three customers for every Jaguar produced. The demand for the E-Type and the Mark 2 was such that a black market existed for the sale of both of these cars, which were bought and sold for considerably more than the Jaguar list price. This must have been frustrating for Sir William Lyons, Jaguar Car's thrifty Chairman and Managing Director, who had worked hard to offer both cars at very competitive prices.

Jaguar was also producing and selling a number of other saloons, albeit in smaller numbers than the Mark 2. One of the problems associated with producing such a wide range of cars was that it was difficult to streamline the production process. These different models did share some common parts, but were also made up of many unique components, which was inefficient and expensive. Another issue was that Jaguar's model ranges were effectively competing against each other in the market place. These included the S-Type and the 420 saloons, which were launched in 1963, as well as the 420G or Mark X, which was launched in 1961 to mixed reviews, including some quite unflattering ones about its styling.

The acquisition by Jaguar of the Daimler Motor Company, largely for its factory space and some would argue their successful commercial vehicles division (which produced, amongst other things, buses and military vehicles), would also give rise to the launch of yet another model in 1962 using the Mark 2 bodyshell. The Daimler 2.5-litre V8 would be Jaguar's first car to be powered by a V8 engine. As this engine was developed by Edward

Turner for Daimler it was not a Jaguar engine; it could more accurately be described as a Daimler engine in a Jaguar bodyshell. Jaguar would not produce their own V8 until the introduction of the AJV8 engine in 1996.

Origins

The development of the XJ saloon began in the early '60s. As early as 1961 Sir William Lyons was working on a car which was at first rather like a stretched E-Type. At Jaguar they were still busy trying to meet demand for the very successful E-Type fixed-head coupé, which had been launched to the press on 15 March 1961 by Sir William Lyons, at a restaurant in the Parc des Eaux Vives. The E-Type being used in the launch, 9600 HP, only just made it with minutes to spare, following a non-stop trip from the factory in Coventry. All the world's press were in attendance in Geneva for the motor show, so it was a perfect time to introduce them to the new E-Type. The launch was paid for by the Society of Motor Manufacturers and Traders. This demonstrated not only great timing for the E-Type's launch by Sir William Lyons, but also his frugality. Not many motor manufacturers have managed to launch a world-beating new model and also have that launch paid for by someone else. The general public thus got to see the E-Type fixed-head coupé for themselves at the Geneva Motor Show, where we know it caused quite a stir.

Work on the XJ began in earnest in 1963 when the Experimental Team were given the task of developing the new Jaguar saloon. The project was initially codenamed XJ4. The XJ prefix stood for Xperimental Jaguar, and the four simply referred to it being the fourth project that the team was working on at the time. It was also interesting to note that while the XK120 was designed in just three days, largely as a test bed for the new XK engine which was destined for the Mark VII, the development process for the XJ took three years.

Introducing MWK 28G

This Jaguar was hand built by the Experimental Team and was registered as being chassis number nineteen of twenty pre-production XJs built. It is recognised as the oldest surviving XJ in the world and it contains many features which make it unique. It was also the first of the XJs to be registered for road use. It is a very important Jaguar, and played a key role in the development of not only the Series 1 XJ, but every XJ that subsequently followed it. *The Telegraph* summed it up by saying, 'It seems to be no more than a very early XJ6 – and only a 2.8-litre model at that – yet there's a case for it being a more important Jaguar than any Le Mans winner.'

MWK 28G was taken to France and Spain in 1968 for extensive road testing by Jonathan Heynes (son of Bill Heynes, Jaguar's Technical Director), an Apprentice Development Engineer, and also by Jim Graham, who was a part of Norman Dewis's Test Driving Team. This is what Jonathan had to say about MWK 28G:

> I worked MWK 28G up into a press car, and it was probably the best of them. In June or July 1968, just a few weeks before the XJ6 was launched, I drove the still-camouflaged MWK 28G out to Le Mans to meet the journalist Michael Sedgwick,

The world's oldest surviving XJ6.

who was borrowing it for a magazine feature. A weld on the exhaust downpipe fractured and we had to get it brazed-up locally, it wasn't a big deal, but typical of the problems we had to deal with on the hoof. We were such a small team, it's amazing how well the car worked out! It really didn't give a lot of trouble.

In 1968, after Jim Graham had driven MWK over to France, he was joined by renowned photojournalist John Finlayson, who met them to document the car's journey through France and into Asturias in northern Spain. During this trip the car spent most of its time rather crudely camouflaged with cardboard, paint and tape. During this trip and for other trips, it was not unusual for MWK to be driven at high speeds for prolonged periods of time, on this occasion in the hot Spanish climate. At no point were there any problems with MWK's 2.8-litre engine, which coped well with everything that it was asked to do.

When they arrived in Leon Jim checked into the local Parador and MWK was carefully hidden out of the sight of prying eyes. As part of the launch publicity for the XJ6, Jaguar had arranged something rather special: a photoshoot with supermodel Veruschka and her boyfriend Franco Rubartelli. Veruschka von Lehndorff was a German aristocrat, model, actress and artist. She was the first German supermodel, and to have her photographed with the new Jaguar was quite a coup. Veruschka and her photographer boyfriend had been regularly featured in all the international editions of *Vogue*.

MWK's Unique Features

The bodyshell and outer panels of MWK 28G were produced for Jaguar by Pressed Steel Fischer and look very much like most other Series 1 XJs. One of the main visual differences between MWK and the XJ saloons that went into production is the bonnet. The 2.8-litre engine has a shorter stroke than its 4.2-litre brother, and didn't need as much room under the bonnet. The production cars had to have a different bonnet pressing, which incorporates a slightly raised centre bonnet section to accommodate the slightly larger engine.

There are a number of differences inside, such as the sill tread plates, which have been hand formed in aluminium and cut using a hacksaw. You have to remove the seat squab to spot another, which is the quite simplistic seat frame construction, which is quite different from production models. This would have been made up by hand. One of the bracing arms under the bonnet and attached to the inner wing is in a slightly different location. This looks, to my eye anyway, slightly better than on my 1973 Daimler Sovereign, where it partially obstructs the rear carburettor dashpot top, which makes topping up with dashpot oil slightly more difficult.

Adrian, the current owner of the world's oldest XJ, has made a few upgrades including the installation of electronic ignition, and (some people might gasp here) changing the rear tailpipes to curved, and then back to straight. Early XJs were manufactured with straight pipes, though they were later changed on the Series 1 XJ to the classic curved pipes, which most people will be familiar with. This was to solve the problem of fumes entering the passenger compartment. This fault seems to be an intermittent one; I know of Series 1 owners with both types of exhaust pipes; some have the straight pipes and don't have any problems, and some have changed theirs because of this issue. PHP42G,

Simple hand-crafted metal seat frame.

Above: The right-hand engine bracing strut, which obscures the rear carburettor dashpot on production models, is in a slightly different position on MWK 28G.

Below: MWK 28G's chassis plate.

which was Sir William Lyons' personal transport, still has the original straight pipes. And, as Adrian will attest, changing the pipes led to no difference in fume levels in his car.

Adrian says 'It's all about drivability for me. I want to be able to use the car, and I believe these are sensible upgrades which allow me to do this.' Adrian is, and always has been, keen to ensure that MWK 28G doesn't spend its life languishing somewhere in a museum. One other change which became necessary is one which most Jaguar owners will have experienced themselves at some point over the years, which is the failure of the headlining. This is caused by the deterioration of the glue that holds the headlining cloth to the backboard. When this happens there is only really one thing that can be done, so MWK's headlining was replaced.

MWK's bonnet pressing has a lower profile than the production cars. It had to be raised to accommodate the 4.2-litre production engine, which sits higher in the engine bay than the 2.8-litre engine.

MKW 28G has the classic Series 1 XJ6 layout with chrome rim dials.

Time to Say Goodbye

As with many of the other cars at Jaguar that have been used for testing and promotional purposes, in June 1970 MWK 28G was sold into private ownership. This may at least be partly due to the prudent way that Sir William Lyons managed Jaguar; he did not like to waste money. MWK 28G had fulfilled its purpose and was no longer required for active duty at Jaguar, so it became an asset that could be realised.

Before it was sold the original 2.8-litre engine (with a mileage of around 20,000 miles) was removed and replaced with a brand-new 2.8-litre engine. There was nothing wrong with the

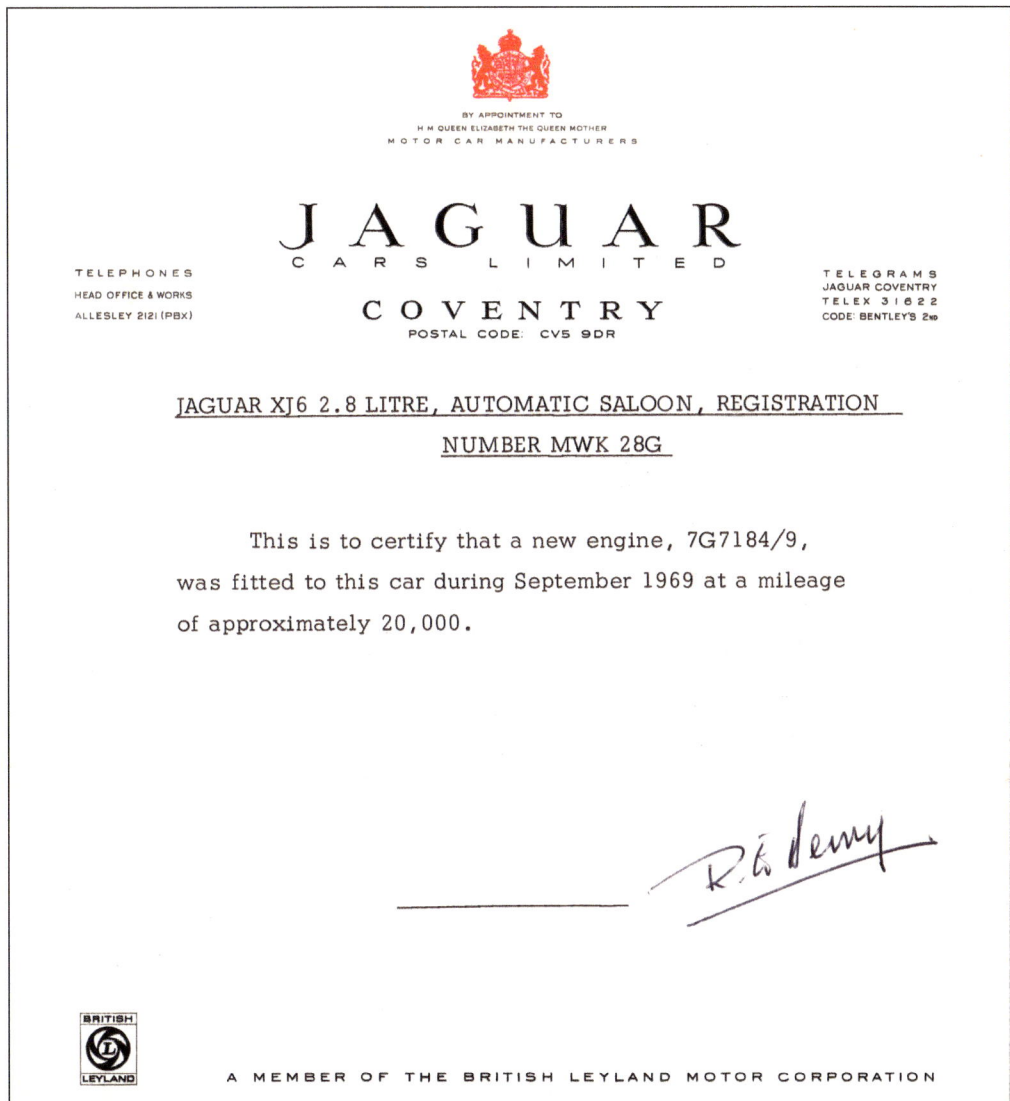

Letter from Jaguar confirming that MWK 28G's engine was changed before being offered for sale.

original engine, which had survived the rigours of extensive testing with no problems. It had in fact been extremely reliable, and had given little trouble throughout its Jaguar life. It was just that it wasn't thought to be good practice to sell a car with a test engine that had done 20,000 miles. The cost of doing this was fairly small for Jaguar, but enabled them to sell the car for a higher price. Thus, MWK cannot really be considered as a matching numbers car, as its original engine had been removed prior to resale. The original bill of sale lists the sale price of MWK 28G as £1,900, just £99 less than the Jaguar list price for a 2.8 automatic at the time. Jaguar were able to sell MWK 28G at this price because demand for the model was still very strong.

MWK 28G's original bill of sale.

An Unfortunate Incident

2018 was a busy year for MWK 28G, as it was also a very important anniversary for the Jaguar XJ in general, being fifty years since its original launch. During the anniversary year, MWK was unsurprisingly much in demand and the car's presence was requested at a number of the celebrations taking place around the country, but also in Europe. It returned to Salamanca, in northern Spain, close to where it had been sent in 1968 for testing and for promotional photos. MWK visited what must be its spiritual home, Sir William Lyons' former home, Wappenbury Hall. The house is around a half-hour's drive from the original

A rather unique rear window sticker for MWK 28G.

MWK has the 2.8-litre engine and a three-speed BorgWarner automatic gearbox.

Jaguar Cars' factory site at Browns Lane, just outside Coventry. MWK also took part in a cavalcade of significant XJs, which drove around the fabled motor racing circuit at Brands Hatch as part of the XJ50 celebrations. There were plenty of magazine articles too, with features in *Jaguar World, Practical Classics* and *Classic Cars*.

The final event of the year for MWK took place in November, at the National Exhibition Centre in Birmingham, at the Lancaster Classic Car Show. MWK 28G was on the Jaguar Enthusiasts Club stand. The show was well attended for the three days it took place, and the world's oldest Jaguar enjoyed a lot of attention. Everything passed without incident until after the show; as things were being packed away, the second loading deck of the transport company's vehicle crashed down onto MWK's roof causing significant damage to the car.

The original early rear screen featured a horizontal heated rear window, with very thin silver wires which were only just visible to the naked eye – and it shattered. These screens are impossible to replace unless you are lucky enough to find a car that still has its original early screen and is being broken for parts. Other damage included the roof being stretched by the impact, which also distorted the D post. The saddest thing about this needless accident was that apart from a small amount of paint being required after wing mirrors added in the 1970s were removed from the car, and a sill and wheel arch repair, the rest of the paint was original and in good condition. There was nothing for it; in view of the damage caused, the whole car would have to be repainted. You cannot put a price on lost originality like that, and although MWK would look fine, it would never be quite the same again.

For over twenty years Keith Parrington at XJ Restorations had kept MWK in tip-top condition. The obvious choice was to entrust this vital to work to Keith and his team at his new company, Painting Classic Cars. All the work was done sympathetically and to

Early cars had the centre of the steel wheels painted in the same colour as the car. MWK also has Sundym glass, which could be because of its continental road-testing beginnings.

Above: The regency red paintwork was carefully matched to MWK 28G's original paint colour.

Below: The oldest XJ meets one of the last Series 1 Daimler Sovereigns produced.

the high standard required, but it must have been rather sad for both Adrian and Keith, who had for many years striven to preserve MWK as it was. Work was carried out as it would have been at the time MWK was originally built, using hammers and dollies, and a small nudge from a hydraulic ram to encourage the D pillar to get back into its original shape. Paint was removed using a specialist tool, an Eastwood SCT. This tool removes paint without damaging the metalwork beneath. Keith commented that the bodywork was 'simply stunning' underneath the paint.

The history of MWK exemplifies nicely the love, care and loyalty these cars inspire in those who own, preserve and drive them. More examples of this are included in the form of the quotes you can read at the start of each chapter of this book.

Series 1 XJ: 1968–1973

My car was bought new from Henley's for cash by my father-in-law, paying a hefty premium to jump the waitlist. It was used extensively in the '70s and '80s, regularly being driven between London and Madrid. It was then semi-retired after being used as our wedding car in Spain in the early '90s. We saved it from being scrapped and have been restoring it on and off for the last twenty years or so, finally getting it back on the road in 2020.

Paul Muncey, owner Series 1 XJ6 4.2-litre manual overdrive

A World Beater Arrives

In 1977, Thames Television's *Drive In* featured a rare interview by Tony Bastable with Sir William Lyons, in which he said that the XJ was his favourite of all the cars that Jaguar had produced, explaining that each car produced by Jaguar should be better than its predecessor. The XJ was the last car where Sir William Lyons was fully involved with all the stages of the development and production process.

In 1968, when the Series 1 XJ6 was finally introduced to the world, it was a very different time from today. There was no internet, no mobile phones and no social media. For this reason, the motoring press played a much more significant part in the introduction and launch of any new model of car. The main titles in 1968, which were published weekly, were *Motor* and *Autocar*. These publications were a potential new owner's main source of information about a new make or model, and a poor review would have been very detrimental to the future success of any car.

We know how important Sir William Lyons felt these reviews and reports were, and that he would often telephone the editor of a magazine that was conducting a road test before publication, to get the heads-up on what was going to appear in print. The following example is a good demonstration of the power of the press and how seriously Jaguar took these road tests and reviews. Sir William had not been happy about an unfavourable review of the Mark X. This particular road test had been conducted by Roger Bell, a staff writer at *Motor*, who had identified what he felt were some shortcomings with the Mark X. Following publication of his article, Roger was invited to Jaguar where he took part in a meeting with Jaguar's engineering executive, who tried to persuade him that his misgivings were incorrect.

It was about this time that Jaguar brought in a meticulous process to ensure that any cars supplied to the press would be in tip-top condition. More attention was given to ensuring that these cars were prepared to an extremely high standard than to any car that ever left the production line at Browns Lane. If Jaguar had produced all their cars this way, with the same level of attention to detail, it is unlikely they would ever have made any profit. But it clearly demonstrates how important Jaguar thought these road tests and reports were to the success of its cars.

It is often said that there was nothing new about the XJ6, and this is at least partially true. The XJ6's independent rear suspension had been used on the S-Type and the 420. The XK engine had been used in many of Jaguar's previous models, although a new variant of this engine, with a smaller capacity, would become part of the range. This 2.8-litre engine was strategically placed to allow it to be specified by company car drivers in countries where they were limited to choosing cars with engines under 3 litres in capacity. The XJ6 did feature an all-new anti-dive front suspension. It also made the most of new technology, which would allow it to almost completely isolate the occupants of the car from all road noise and vibration.

What is not mentioned often is that never before had such a complete package been offered in the form of the XJ6. It took all the best bits that Jaguar had been using in their other cars and brought them together in one very well-rounded package. This new gold standard was to set the benchmark which other manufacturers would have to strive to reach for some time. Even manufacturers like Rolls-Royce would ignore the XJ6 at their peril. The importance of the XJ6 cannot be overstated. It would in time go on to replace the rest of the Jaguar production models apart from the E-Type and the Daimler DS420 Limousine. The DS420 was introduced in April 1968, and was manufactured at the Vanden Plas coachworks in London using the floorpan from the Mark X, also sharing a number of other parts.

To put it plainly, the success and survival of Jaguar was resting on the XJ6. Sir William Lyons had placed his eggs firmly in the XJ6 basket, and for Jaguar to flourish it just had to be a success. I am sure that Sir William knew that he had a world beater on his hands, but what would the motoring press of the time have to say? He certainly had no need to worry because the reception that the new XJ6 received was rapturous to say the least. *Motor* magazine from the week ending 10 May 1969 was typical of the praise that would be heaped upon Jaguar's latest arrival.

They tested a 4.2-litre car with a manual overdrive gearbox and found very little to criticise and much to praise. The comprehensive six-page report contained a wealth of technical information and observations about the car. They start their report by noting how long it had taken them to get hold of an XJ6 for testing purposes, and suggesting that their report would only increase the demand that Jaguar was already struggling to fulfil. But they also told prospective owners with their names on the waiting list for an XJ6 to be patient, because the XJ6 would be well worth the wait.

The Series 1 XJ6 looks good in most colours, but silver seems to particularly suit its feline curves. Shown here with the optional Square 8 Lucas fog lights.

The four-headlight arrangement had been a feature of Jaguars for some time. Replacing the fake air intakes with the optional fog lights gives the car a sportier feel.

The car is fitted with a four-speed manual gearbox, which has overdrive on fourth gear, effectively offering five gears.

4.2-litre badging on the Series 1 XJ6.

4.2-litre engine bay, straight six DOHC engine with twin HS8 carburettors; the automatic enrichment device AED sits between the carburettors. Unusually number 1 piston is at the rear of the engine.

Series 1 XJ6 with a sumptuous red leather interior.

As a celebration of the XJ6, Jaguar themselves produced a book containing a selection of the glowing reports from the motoring pundits of the day, entitled *Jaguar XJ6 praise indeed...* In the introduction to this publication, it stated that,

> We doubt if any car has received such unqualified praise as the XJ6 from both the technical and general press, and the extracts contained in this booklet convey its outstanding merit in every respect of automobile design.

In the Comparison Tests section, Jim Mosen from his *Motor* report of 21 March 1970 compared the XJ6 to a Rolls-Royce.

One comparative road test pitted the 4.2-litre XJ6 against BMW's 3.0S. The price comparison was interesting. The BMW retailed at £3,652 including £114 for the optional power steering, and Jaguar came in at £2,926. It should be remembered that this situation would be reversed outside the UK due to exchange rates and trade tariffs, and that the Jaguar in an export market would have become the more expensive car. Both cars featured an in-line straight six engine with an aluminium head and a cast-iron block. The test concluded that at £726 more, the BMW was not worth the extra outlay. The tester, David Thomas, felt that the BMW was more of a drivers' car, but in contrast he also stated that the Jaguar was definitely the quieter and more comfortable ride.

This is not to say that the Series 1 XJ6 was faultless. Some people felt that the steering was too light and offered only limited 'road feel', particularly at higher speeds. This was because the amount of assistance gained from the power steering was not variable according to the speed of the vehicle. In an interview conducted by Dave Stewart, which was filmed in the back of his Series 2 XJ12, former Jaguar test driver Norman Dewis

> "Not only is the XJ6 far and away the best saloon that Jaguar have ever made—and their standards have always been high—but we believe that in its behaviour it gets closer to overall perfection than any other luxury car we have yet tested, regardless of price."
>
> *Motor 10th May 1969*

A quote from the book produced by *Jaguar XJ6, praise indeed...* This was a compilation made up from press and magazine reports on the Series 1 XJ6.

> "It may not be a Rolls-Royce but if ever a car did everything as well as a Rolls and a lot of things much better then it is the XJ6 . . . at one-third of the price."

Also from *Jaguar XJ6, praise indeed...* In this comment the Rolls-Royce Siver Shadow comes in for some criticism.

explained the reason behind the choice of very light power steering. He related that it was because Sir William Lyons had decided that to be successful in the American market it needed to have power steering that could be operated with one finger, because this was what the American market liked and demanded from their cars. This shows the perceived importance of the American market both to Sir William Lyons and Jaguar.

Not All Plain Sailing

The 2.8-litre engine had behaved faultlessly during extensive, rigorous and arduous road testing. It was worked hard and driven for prolonged periods at high speed, but on the road it developed an unexpected problem. In the real world where customers drove more sedately, at considerably lower speeds for shorter distances, this smaller engine could develop quite a specific problem. Carbon deposits, which were burnt off at higher speeds or if the engine was worked harder, accumulated on the crown (top) of the pistons causing an extensive build-up of heat, which resulted in pistons being holed. The problem was being dealt with by the customer service team at Jaguar, and many of the team members had a holed piston on their desks, which they used as pen holders.

This was, to the say the least, unfortunate, because the smaller 2.8-litre engine, which can rev more freely and operate at substantially higher speeds than the 4.2-litre engine, is said by many to run more sweetly than its bigger 4.2-litre brother. A testament to this is the number of 2.8-litre cars that are still around. Originally 2.8-litre car sales accounted for about a third of overall Series 1 XJ6 sales. Following some improvements this engine has proved to be as reliable as the 4.2-litre engine.

The engine-related problems have affected resale values, although there are now many fans of the 2.8-litre engine among Series 1 XJ6 owners. The smaller engine does not fare as well when it is offered with the three-speed Borg-Warner automatic transmission. Its performance is certainly not as impressive as its larger-capacity brother, but when it is mated to a manual overdrive gearbox, with the Laycock overdrive on fourth gear, it is very much a Jaguar. It can be driven enthusiastically and at the same time is a rewarding car to drive.

Some changes were made to the 2.8-litre engine following the problems experienced by customers. These problems included pistons holing and piston ring damage, noisy timing chains (broken slipper pad), and failure of the rear main oil seal often accompanied by the rear main bearing showing blueing. Normally these would occur outside the warranty period of twelve months or 12,000 miles. Another problem was the failure of the brake servo vacuum pipe which collapsed internally due to fuel vapour damage. This problem was fixed by a factory modification to the pipe.

The 4.2-litre cars had a few problems too. There were some big end failures with conrod penetration through both sides of the engine block. There were coolant loss issues caused by head gasket failures, and engine blocks which were subject to cracking between some of the bores. Customers reported fumes entering the passenger cabin, which Jaguar initially tried to solve by trying to more effectively seal the passenger cabin from fume ingress. But the solution to this problem was far more straightforward and complaints were largely eradicated with the adoption of the S-shaped tailpipes. They curved outwards from the car, taking fumes away from the passenger cabin and into the vehicle's slipstream to be carried away.

Both the 2.8-litre cars and 4.2-litre cars suffered from exhaust problems. The mild steel exhaust systems were prone to rotting, particularly the rear silencers. This was often attributed to the petrol specification at the time and was thought to be more prevalent on cars that made more short local journeys. This was because for short runs the automatic choke would operate during the warm-up of the car, resulting in the fuel mixture being richer, and therefore causing a build-up of carbon from unburned fuel.

The Official Launch

The XJ6 was launched in London at the Earls Court Motor Show on 10 October 1968. As with previous Jaguar models, the entry-level 2.8-litre car was extremely competitively priced at £1,897. As reviewers of the day and Sir William Lyons were keen to point out, the new Jaguar XJ6 offered previously unavailable levels of ride and comfort at a bargain basement price when compared to other manufacturers of the day including Rolls-Royce.

The advertising featured a photo of Sir William Lyons standing behind an XJ6. In the text he says, 'In the long history of Jaguar this is the very first time that I have featured in an advertisement for one of our cars. But it seems only right that I should personally introduce the XJ6 to you.' He goes on to say, 'I believe the XJ6 is the finest saloon car that Jaguar have ever made, and one that challenges comparison with any in the world.' When the XJ6 was featured at the Paris Motor Show, Sir William Lyons would personally demonstrate his newest creation to President de Gaulle.

Officially three models were available at launch: a standard saloon with the 2.8-litre engine, a 2.8-litre De Luxe saloon and a 4.2-litre saloon. It would be almost a year before Daimler fans would get their own model, a Daimler Sovereign, which would be available with either a 2.8-litre engine or a 4.2-litre engine. Owners of both Jaguars and Daimlers could specify either the three-speed Borg-Warner automatic transmission or a manual overdrive gearbox with a Laycock overdrive on fourth gear, effectively making it a five-speed gearbox. In 1972 it was announced that the V12 engine would be joining the line-up of available engines. A year earlier this variant had been made available as an option on the E-Type. Now the range comprised of Jaguars and Daimlers with either the 2.8-litre straight six, the 4.2-litre straight six, or the 5.3-litre V12. There was also a top-of-the-range model, the Vanden Plas, which had the highest-level specification of all the cars. The Series 1 XJ12 and the Daimler Double Six Vanden Plas were the ultimate Jaguar models. With a top speed of around 150 mph, at the time the XJ12 held the record for the fastest production car available in the world.

In response to customers' requests for an increase in legroom for rear seat passengers, the XJ chassis was extended by 4 inches. At this point both short wheelbase (SWB) and long wheelbase (LWB) versions became available. For a while it was possible to choose which wheelbase you preferred. The feeling generally is that the SWB chassis is the ultimate chassis for the XJ, but rear seat passengers might disagree, and eventually the standard became the LWB chassis. The coupé continued to use the SWB chassis, but due

The Daimler Sovereign was launched in 1969, a year later than its Jaguar counterpart, and sported the traditional Daimler fluted bonnet grille and a chrome strip running through the centre of the bonnet.

The fluted boot plinth and Sovereign badging told everyone that this was a Daimler. As this is a later Series 1, the reversing lights are clear and there is a separate reflector below the tail lights. Early cars had the reflectors built into the reversing lights.

Above: The engine bay of the Daimler Sovereign was similar to its Jaguar stablemate, but the engine sported a Daimler decal on the cam cover.

Below: The Daimler seats had a wider pleat than the Jaguars, which were narrower and perforated; headrests were optional. Some said that the leather used in the Daimlers was of superior quality to the Jaguars. Only the Jaguars had the wooden door cappings; the Daimlers were vinyl.

The Series 1 V12 bonnet grille which is favoured by many Series 1 fans over the standard XJ6 grille.

Still sporting its original Australian registration plate, this Series 1 XJ12 is as good underneath as it looks on top.

Above: Not many XJ12s have matching boot badges and number plates.

Below: An engine bay to die for. The V12 engine always looks like it has been shoe-horned in compared to the XJ6, but which one would you rather work on?

A tachometer that red-lines at 6,500 rpm and a speedometer that goes up to 160 mph means just one thing: you are looking at an XJ12 dashboard.

to the changeover of wheelbase on the saloon there were a very limited number of LWB Series 1 cars built, along with a few SWB Series 2 cars.

In 1973, after five years in production, the XJ was due for a refresh, to help it to continue to compete against the offerings from other motor manufacturers of the day. There was also a need to respond to the changing regulations affecting saloon cars in other parts of the world, particularly in America.

Series 2 XJ: 1973–1979

I bought my Jag around seven years ago as a non-runner from a chap in Lancashire. I have had several other classic cars but this is my first and, so far, only Jag. It was in honour of my grandfather who used to own them and my fond childhood memories of riding around in an XJ6. It was only after I bought it that I realised it had first been registered to a Kennings dealership in Buxton where I had moved from my native West Yorkshire in the same year. It's quite possible I would have seen it in the showroom window back in 1976. Great coincidence and some personal provenance for me. With the help of friends and a commercial garage owner it's being (and continues to be) restored and, more importantly, enjoyed.

Julian Collis, owner Series 2 XJ6 3.4-litre manual overdrive

Times Are a Changing

After five years of the Series 1 XJ, in which time 98,527 Series 1 XJ6s and XJ12s had been produced, it was time for a change. This change was largely led by new safety regulations that were being introduced in Jaguar's biggest overseas market, the United States. This market was very important to Jaguar; Sir William Lyons closely followed developments in the American car market, and was often guided by the trends that were established there. For example, previous American safety legislation had reduced the size of the XJ's two fuel tanks from 11 to 10 gallons.

Extensive changes were needed to the Series 1 to create the Series 2 XJ. Externally the front bumper height was raised to meet the new American safety regulations and through necessity the radiator grille became smaller and less prominent. Impact protection was improved and internally the passenger doors were given side impact bars. The front bulkhead was redesigned and strengthened, effectively virtually sealing off the passenger compartment from the engine bay.

Fibre optic lighting was introduced for the first time and the sometimes-criticised heating and ventilation system from the Series 1 XJ was replaced by a fully functioning air-conditioning system. The fibre optic system was quite state of the art at the time, and

Above: American specification Series 2 XJ12, with bumpers modified to meet American safety legislation. (Photo courtesy of Scott Docie)

Below: American specification Series 2 XJ12, looking good against its Florida backdrop at Palm Beach. (Photo courtesy of Scott Docie)

American specification Series 2 XJ12. The interior of the XJ12 features the Daimler-style wider-pleated seating. (Photo courtesy of Scott Docie)

this was the first time that a system of this type had been used on a production car, as previously it had only been used in medical equipment. It relied on a single central bulb which fed light through fibre optic cables to all the areas that needed illumination. In fact, when the cars were new you could tie the fibre optic cable in a knot and the light would still get through.

The interior layout changed considerably, and the Series 2 got a new revised dashboard that would see the demise of the centrally located bank of gauges with the row of rocker switches underneath, which had been a feature of the Series 1 XJ. These gauges would be replaced by the vents for the new air-conditioning system. The new gauges were moved to a position in front of the driver and these included a rev counter, a speedometer, an oil pressure gauge, a volt meter, a fuel gauge and a temperature gauge. This was more in line with what other manufacturers were doing with the gauges in their own cars. The windscreen wiper and washer controls moved from the central section of the dashboard and were now placed on a stalk to the side of the steering wheel; this was also more in line with what other manufacturers of the time were doing. The windscreen wipers also got a single wipe function, and the headlight main beam dipswitch moved from its position in the driver's footwell to the steering column, where it was operated by a push function on the wiper stalk.

The much-maligned 2.8-litre XK engine would continue to be part of the engine options offered for the Series 2 XJ until April 1975, when it would be replaced by an all-new 3.4-litre XK engine. The 2.8-litre was not a popular engine choice and only 170 Series 2 XJs were produced. It never really did get over its reputation for holing pistons, and even today this is reflected in the value of the 2.8-litre engine XJs.

A little surprisingly, the 3.4-litre XJ would never be offered in LWB format and would only be available as SWB. Perhaps this was because it was seen as the entry-level car, and this helped to differentiate it from the rest of the range. It might also have been that it was aimed at the fleet car market. It would be offered badged as either a Jaguar or a Daimler Sovereign. The switch to the LWB chassis happened gradually for the saloon after the launch of the Series 2 XJ, but by the end of 1974 all saloons would be LWB. The SWB floorpan would continue to be used for the XJ-S. When the Series 2 range was introduced, it was announced that it would be made up of the 2.8-litre saloon (only available as an XJ6), the 4.2-litre saloon,

Right: The 3.4-litre engine replaced the 2.8-litre engine, and this model was only ever available with carburettors and in SWB form.

Below: This front view clearly shows the revised front bumper height and the shallower grille.

Still very much a Jaguar, a car that looks like it is moving when its stationary.

It may have been the entry-level car but it wouldn't look out of place at your country estate.

The Series 1 XJ6 lets the Series 2 XJ6 take the lead.

the 5.3-litre V12 and the XJ-C. The coupé would not make it into the XJ range for a further two years, which would see it being launched in the same year as the XJ-S. As well as a Jaguar version of all the above cars, a Daimler Sovereign variant was also available. Finally, there were two Vanden Plas options: the top-of-the-range Daimler Double Six Vanden Plas and the 4.2-litre Daimler Vanden Plas.

Turbulent Times

The Series 2 XJ was launched during a rather turbulent time for the British motor industry. One of the reasons behind Sir William Lyons' original merger with the British Motor Corporation (BMC, after which they became known as British Motor Holdings) in 1968 was to protect Jaguar from potential acquisition by other motor manufacturers. A number of other British manufacturers had disappeared following acquisitions of this sort, and initially, at least, Sir William was able to maintain full control of Jaguar. Despite following the American market quite closely, Sir William wanted Jaguar to remain in British hands. He realised that the future would see there being far fewer motor manufacturers overall, and he had seen other groups of companies like the Rootes Group disappear as they were slowly absorbed by the American company Chrysler.

Sir William was not getting any younger, and after the tragic death of his son, John, while driving to the 1955 Le Mans twenty-four-hour race, he had no clear successor. Sir William's style of charismatic micromanagement did not make the development of a management successor particularly straightforward. The joint statement issued to announce the merger promised Jaguar 'the greatest practical degree of autonomy under the Chairmanship of Sir William Lyons'. However, this was easier to promise than deliver, and when British Motor Holdings subsequently merged with Leyland Holdings in 1968, forming the British Leyland Motor Corporation, it became much harder for Jaguar to maintain independent control.

Sales Remain Strong

Despite problems with poor build quality and supply problems, the Series 2 Jaguars continued to sell well, and production figures for the Series 2 surpassed those of the Series 1. A total of 127,961 Series 2s were built, 29,434 more than the Series 1. The high demand for the XJ continued and Jaguar once again struggled to produce enough cars to meet customer demand. At the launch of the Series 2 XJ range the average customer wait time was around twelve months. Jaguar were working hard to increase production, but with Jaguar estimating that the weekly build rate could be increased from its highest ever level of 750 cars produced in September 1973 to around 850 to 900 vehicles per week, the backlog would still take years to clear.

The most popular choice of Series 2 car was the XJ6 L fitted with the 4.2-litre engine – 57,804 of these were sold. Next in line was the XJ12 L, 16,010 of which were sold. Not

The Daimler Sovereign retained its trademark fluted grille and a chrome strip down the centre of the bonnet.

As with other Daimlers the Series 2 cars also featured the Daimler D on their hub caps.

The air vent below the front bumper was more pronounced than on the Series 1 XJ.

The Daimler Sovereign was never sold in the United States because Jaguar did not have the rights to use the Daimler name there.

The Daimler engine bay. The 4.2-litre XK engine is fuelled using twin SU HIF7 carburettors. These carburettors were also used on the Daimler Limousine.

Luxurious interior of the Series 2 Daimler Sovereign.

Improvements aimed at making the dashboard area more driver friendly saw the gauges move into the area immediately behind the steering wheel.

much further behind that was the Daimler Sovereign 4.2-litre, with 14,531 sales. At the bottom of the sales table was the 2.8-litre XJ with just 107 cars sold. The 3.4-litre proved to be a much more popular choice with over 9,000 cars being sold for the Jaguar and Daimler variants. Cost-wise the SWB 4.2-litre Jaguar XJ6 was the best value at £3,674. Adding that all-important 4 extra inches of legroom for rear seat passengers would set you back another £450. The two most expensive options were the Daimler Double Six coupé at £6,131 and the Daimler Double Six Vanden Plas at £7,333. This was almost double the cost of the cheapest Series 2 XJ but, despite this, 1,726 people purchased Jaguar's top-of-the-range XJ flagship.

The performance of the 2.8-litre automatic Series 2 XJ was the slowest of the XJ range, reaching 60 mph in 11.0 seconds. The 3.4-litre XJ was one tenth of a second quicker at 10.9 seconds. The 4.2-litre XJ got to 60 mph in 8.9 seconds, which was just one tenth of a second slower than its Series 1 counterpart. This was probably not the LWB version however, because that extra 4 inches of chassis added an additional 50 kg of weight. An auto test report carried out by *Autocar* in October 1974 confirms this. The 8.8 seconds time of the Series 1 4.2-litre XJ had dropped to 10.3 seconds for the Series 2. It also noted that the top speed of the Series 1 XJ, which was 124 mph, had dropped to 116 mph for the Daimler Sovereign. Comparative vehicles of the time, such as the BMW 3.3L, had a higher top speed of 124 mph and a quicker 0–60 mph time of 9.9 seconds. But all this came at a considerable price increase, and at £8,443 the BMW was £3,643 more expensive than the Daimler Sovereign.

The only more competitively priced car that was tested also came from British Leyland (British Leyland Motor Corporation), and was the Rover 3500 V8. It was priced at £3,168, and as such was £1,632 less than the Daimler Sovereign. The Rover had a lower top speed of 112 mph and a 0–60 time of 10.8 seconds, half a second slower than the Daimler Sovereign. The most expensive car in this test, the Rolls-Royce Silver Shadow at £12,204, was £7,404 more expensive than the Daimler Sovereign. The Rolls-Royce was faster at 119 mph, but only one tenth of a second faster to 60 mph. Purchasing the top-of-the-range Daimler Double Six for £7,333 (almost £5,000 cheaper than the Rolls-Royce Silver Shadow) would have delivered a top speed of 147 mph and a 0–60 time of 7.8 seconds, and better fuel economy. This is also true of the BMW 3.3L, which at £8,443 was still over a thousand pounds more than the flagship Daimler Double Six.

In the luxury car market Jaguars and Daimlers really did represent excellent value for money. A buyer would not have to compromise on engineering excellence; they would get one the world's best production V12 engines. So even if the build quality of the Series 2 was known to be variable at times, it still offered a world-beating package. However, the Daimler Sovereign was amongst the thirstiest of the cars tested, at around 14.3 miles per gallon; only the Rolls-Royce Silver Shadow at 12.4 miles per gallon did worse.

What's the Value of My XJ?

Many people are interested in the value of their XJ. However, a brief description will not suffice for their car to be accurately valued. The simplest answer is that it is worth whatever someone will pay you for it. It is important not to be confused by insurance valuations, as these are often owner valuations, and cars are usually insured for more than their market value. When trying to value any classic car, a very useful starting point is Practical Classic's *Classic Car Price Guide*. They have done all the legwork and keep regular tabs on what cars actually sell for, by looking at clubs, auctions and trade advertisements, online and in print. They update their price guide regularly too. These guides do not list the complete model range for all manufacturers, so not all the models produced by Jaguar will be included.

Values go out of date quite quickly, though some trends over time can be observed. For example, because the 2.8-litre XJ6 engine was not free of issues, those problems continue to be reflected in resale prices to this day. Though of course, the higher-performance engines might simply be more sought after. Currently the highest prices are for the coupés, which now command very strong resale values. Of the Series 1, 2 and 3 XJs, the Series 1 has the strongest prices with the 4.2-litre cars outperforming the 2.8-litre cars by around 50 per cent. Despite the Daimler Sovereign being the more expensive car to purchase originally, and having a higher-quality interior, the Jaguar XJs had always had a better resale value. That has recently changed, and now for the first time (that I have noticed) Series 1 Daimler Sovereign resale prices are higher than those of their Jaguar counterparts.

To start to value any classic car you need to see it and drive it. Even the same make and model can feel very different once you get behind the wheel, due to the owners having spent all the hard-earned cash on the shiny coat of paint on top rather than the very important underpinnings. Similarly, some cars that could never be described as lookers drive beautifully, because all the important bits are as they should be.

More By Luck Than Judgment

The Series 2 XJ continued the excellent work of the Series 1. It was well liked and sold well around the world. But there were problems. In the world beyond the factory gates, the price of oil had risen by 300 per cent by the end of 1973. This rise had been orchestrated by the Organization of Arab Petroleum Exporting Countries, who imposed oil embargos against a number of countries including the UK. This led to a three-day working week and petrol rationing was seriously considered, but in the end was narrowly avoided as the crisis lessened. By the end of 1974 the $3 dollar per barrel crude oil price of early 1973 had risen to $15 per barrel, leading to customers looking to smaller and less thirsty imported cars, encouraged by the UK's recent joining of the European Union. Strong demand for the Series 2, enhanced by its very competitive pricing, helped minimize the impact of external conditions. But for how long could that last?

For this was not the only problem facing Jaguar. The build quality was so poor that, for example, in Japan dealers could sometimes spend up to £2,000 preparing a car to make it ready for sale. The dealers often absorbed part of this cost themselves. The problem was not limited to Jaguars but was part of a systemic problem throughout British Leyland. Cars were leaving the production line with peeling paint, poor fitting trim, and headlining that had fallen down and was touching the seats.

British Leyland was damaging the reputation of Jaguar by exacerbating slipshod work practices, poor quality control, and ineffective management of the Jaguar workforce. It was a situation that would have to change if Jaguar were to survive. Once again there was a huge amount at stake, and by 1977 they needed a new model to replace the ageing Series 2 XJ. It was going to be a very tall order for the Series 3 XJ to accomplish this. Not only did Jaguar desperately need this new model but the company was going to have to undergo radical change if Jaguar were to be able to compete with other car manufacturers around the world.

XJ-C: 1975–1977

It all started when I was but a boy, four years old to be exact. My dad went out one day in our Ford Cortina GXL (two door, Daytona Yellow), only to return in a Lavender Blue S1 XJ6 2.8 litre with a manual overdrive gearbox. Must have made a deep lasting impression. Not only did I end up owning a DD6 Coupé, but two Series 3 XJ12s, along with at least five examples of the XJ's GT sister. I also ended up working for Jaguar for 21 years, and I was a supplier for two before that. It has been said rip my head off and it says Jaguar, in green of course, just like a stick of rock.

Simon Currell, owner Daimler Double Six 5.3-litre coupé manual

Late to the Party

Originally it was hoped that the XJ-C would be launched in 1973, but production problems held back its launch until 1975. It would then have a relatively short production run until 1977. The short production run and the rather lukewarm reception that the XJ-C received have since made it one of the most desirable of the XJs produced, with the Daimler Double Six being the most sought after of the XJ-C range. With only 403 leaving Browns Lane, this is also the rarest of the XJ-Cs.

The XJ-C was based on the same chassis that was used for the Series 1 XJ6, and this SWB chassis would continue to be used for the XJ-C throughout its production run. This was a considerable time after the use of the SWB chassis had been discontinued for the rest of the XJ saloon range. The XJ-C would also be the last in a long line of Jaguars to have traditional chrome bumpers and later models would use stainless steel instead.

Sir William Lyons was known to observe the trends set by American manufacturers quite closely. In America at the time, the coupé or pillarless-bodied car was proving a popular body style with the American motoring public. All the major manufacturers produced a coupé: Ford had the Mustang, General Motors had the Camaro, and the American Motors Corporation had the Javelin. As far back as November 1966 Sir William was looking at the sales figures for these pillarless-bodied cars in America for 1965. At this point total sales had reached over 4 million units. His official biography notes, 'This was almost double the

The 4.2-litre Daimler coupé with the 5.3-litre Daimler Double Six coupé. Note the Kent alloys on the Daimler Double Six.

Vinyl roofs were standard on the coupés. This one also has a full-length Tudor Webasto sunroof. These were not fitted at the factory but cars were sent from the factory to have them installed. This is not surprising, as this is a coach-built sunroof which is made to measure for the car it is being fitted to.

The Daimler Double Six first appeared in the 1920s and was used to describe a Daimler model's engine. The Double Six nomenclature was revived for the XJ range.

The coupé has an extended and strengthened rear roof pillar which is much thicker than the one on the saloon cars. This is needed to give the car the structural rigidity that was required once the central pillar had been removed.

sales of four-door sedans, five times that of two-door sedans and station wagons and more than eight times that of convertibles. Thoughts turned to a two door pillarless XJ.'

In the battle to gain export sales, adding a coupé to Jaguar's range would have seemed like a sensible option to Sir William Lyons. As he retired at the age of seventy-one in 1972, he would not see the coupé reach production, which must have been a disappointment for him.

Above: American specification Californian XJ6C with side indicators on the front wings. (Photo courtesy of Scott Docie)

Below: American specification Californian XJ6C with American-style rear bumper and round rear reflectors. (Photo courtesy of Scott Docie)

American specification Californian XJ6C. Another chance for a close-up view of the enlarged rear roof pillar and the glassless window aperture. (Photo courtesy of Scott Docie)

American specification Californian XJ6C. Jaguar interior with the narrower pleated leather seats, in contrast to the Daimler seats, which have a much wider pleat. (Photo courtesy of Scott Docie)

The One That Got Away ... Almost

In 1969, a project which had the code name of XJ33/34 led to the construction of a Series 1 XJ-C prototype. It used a rejected 2.8-litre bodyshell that had previously been destined for shipment to Sweden. This bodyshell was sent to the Body Development Shop where under the supervision of Harry Rogers and his team of fabricators the bodyshell underwent some drastic and dramatic changes, which would see it being transformed into a Series 1 XJ-C.

As part of this transformation, it would get a new roof featuring two much wider rear pillars, which would add strength to the bodyshell. The central pillar and the doors were all removed and a new half-height central post was located 3 inches further back. The new post was held in place by a frame which was made up of welded and rivetted steel bars. The rear wing line was moved forward and a section of door skin was fitted over the new framework. The front doors were lengthened using a section taken from another door skin. The glass inside the door was modified too and was tinted and curved. A substantial sheet of steel was positioned behind the rear seats and was held in place by rivets, presumably to stop any flexing.

This XJ-C became a fully working coupé which would act as test bed for many different variations during its life with Jaguar. It would be fitted with a number of different XK engines and would also have a V12 engine fitted long before that engine became available in the E-Type. For a time, it would also be used to evaluate the quad cam V12 engine. It would also be fitted with the five-speed Jaguar gearbox designed by Harry Munday that would sadly never make it into production. It is interesting to speculate what might have happened if it had been launched at the same time as the Series 1 XJ12 in 1973 and had been offered with a V12 engine and a five-speed Jaguar gearbox.

The coupé still bears testament to its previous life at Jaguar and contains a number of largely hidden reminders of this past, such as the remnants of a previously fitted V12 wiring loom and a modified bell housing. Some of the clues to this coupé's past are easier to spot, such as a number of trim pieces that have a distinctly homemade look to them and, as with MWK 28G, a number of metal pieces that still have the hacksaw marks on them, giving away their handmade past. Its final configuration would be with a 4.2-litre XK engine and a manual overdrive four-speed gearbox.

It must have been a lot of fun to be an apprentice at Jaguar at this time, because they would get to use this prototype coupé to run errands around the factory site. The removal of the front passenger seat allowed them to use the coupé to carry the gas bottles used in welding. The factory site was vast and having the apprentices use the coupé to ferry things between departments and buildings saved time and money. As we know the effective use of resources was dear to Sir William Lyons' heart.

Sir William approved the finished Jaguar XJ-C himself; he had followed its progress from the drawing board to prototype. Once he had a working coupé, he then tried to gain the funding required from British Leyland that would allow it to be brought into full production. Those funds were not forthcoming, and this rather special coupé was subsequently hidden away. Its existence was largely a secret, with only a handful of people knowing anything about it. Ron Beaty, who was at the factory at the time of the

XJ-C's production, recalled that one day the car had rolled down a slope and demolished a shed. Fortunately, it only sustained a small amount of damage, which would later be rediscovered during the car's restoration, when the filler in its roof (which had been crudely used to repair it) was removed and the roof was pushed back into its original shape.

After being given a chassis number, so the coupé could be registered in 1977, it was sent to a local scrapyard in Coventry owned by Les Harvey, with instructions that it should be crushed. This is where the story should have ended, had it not been for the owner of that scrapyard, who chose to ignore these instructions. I suspect his motivation was purely monetary, with the prototype coupé being privately sold to a gentleman in Staffordshire, one Edward Loveland. Edward registered the coupé for road use in 1980 and it was given the registration XJA 6. He sold it a month later to Ian Foster.

Ian put the XJ-C in his shed and set about changing its appearance to that of a Series 3 XJ-C. This transformation involved him removing the bonnet as well as the front wings and the front and rear bumpers. Series 3 door handles were crudely added to the car's doors. The car was also treated to a respray in British Racing Green. This new coat of

Heavily disguised as a Series 3 coupé, it is hard to recognise this prototype Series 1 XJC. (Photo courtesy of Adam Rukawai Wright)

two-pack paint was applied on top of the coupé's original paint. The car was then taken to a number of Jaguar Driver's Club events and at no point was anyone any the wiser about this prototype coupé's true identity. It was just accepted as a being a modified XJ-C. Ian even tried to find out more about the car's history by contacting the Jaguar factory by letter. But at this time the Jaguar factory was struggling under the weight of British Leyland, and his efforts proved fruitless. The story gets a little complicated here. I had heard that the XJ-C was sold to a car dealership, who then went bankrupt, and the coupé found itself in the hands of this businesses' London liquidators. But in his April 2000 article for *Jaguar World* Jim Patten reported that the recession of the late 1980s found the coupé, which was by this time part of a large private collection, being put up for sale. It stood out from the other cars in the collection, which consisted of various marques including Ferrari, Aston Martin, Lancia and Jaguar. This slightly strange coupé looked like a Series 3 car but had a Series 1 dash inside, which had been covered in tasteful black vinyl. Jim talked to Ron Beaty, who was able to confirm the car's true identity.

At the time Jim already had a sizeable collection of his own, so passed on the chance to own this prototype coupé. Instead, in a chance conversation that he was having with an Australian coupé fan, Les Hughes, he mentioned the car. Les knew that there had

Undergoing a sympathetic restoration. (Photo courtesy of Adam Rukawai Wright)

been a Series 1 XJ-C prototype, but was surprised to hear that the car had survived. It was purchased by him in 1990. Such was his passion for the XJ-C that he purchased it without even seeing a photo and had it shipped off to Brisbane. Les was not just a fan of the XJ-C but he also had a number of other significant Jaguars, such as a Series 2 XJ12 which was chassis number 1. The coupé was in a rather sorry state when it arrived, and its new owner feared the worst when they spotted that the BRG paint was peeling. Fortunately, this wasn't rust as was first thought, but the original paint had reacted with the paint that was applied directly on top of it, causing extensive micro blistering all over the car.

We now fast forward to 1992 when the coupé was treated to a full sympathetic restoration by one of Australia's top restorers. This XJ-C prototype had only clocked up 4,000 miles in its life so far, something that was confirmed by the condition of the car's mechanical components. Fortunately, the previous owner's attempts to transform it into a Series 3 XJ-C were fairly easy to undo. The restoration took full account of the car's provenance. Under the car's blistering paint it was found to be in excellent order, and showed all the imperfections that came from it being a handmade vehicle. These were all kept and the front wings of the car were changed back to Series 1 wings. The filler was removed from the dent in the roof, and the dent was pushed gently back into its original pre-shed-demolishing position.

The prototype's roof was flatter than the production coupé's, and this coupé's doors are an inch shorter than those of the production cars. The back seats of this prototype are also narrower than those of the production models. The restorers were helped by a change in circumstances at Jaguar, who were now not only more aware of, but also keen to preserve their past, and original drawings and transparencies of the coupé became available. Les didn't do much with the newly restored car, and only once during his ownership was it brought out of hiding. But it was well looked after and remained in excellent condition.

For almost five years the coupé was advertised in a number of Jaguar magazines, but having failed to attract a new owner the car was destined to go to auction at Australia's largest car auction house. Just before it was due to go, Adam Rukawai Wright contacted Les via email and made an offer for the coupé. Adam's initial offer was rejected but in the end a price was agreed. The coupé then spent the next three to four years at Roadbend, an independent family-owned Jaguar specialist that had been started in 1965 by Jim and Betty Percival. It's still a family-run business and today, the three Percival brothers and their sister – Tony, Graham, John and Lindsay – continue to run the company. The coupé remained on display there with a number of other Jaguars which were also owned by Adam. Anyone lucky enough to attend the regular Jag meets there got the chance to see the car. These days this important XJ-C is garaged by Adam, who now has purpose-built storage for all his Jaguars. He was invited and has taken part in the 'Celebration of the Motorcar', Australia's premier invitation-only car event.

When time allows, Adam hopes to tour Australia in his unique coupé and help to educate people about its existence and to understand its significance in the development of the XJ-C, the XJ Series of cars, and Jaguar itself.

The speedometer is still showing a mileage of just under 6,000 miles – not bad for a car that is close to fifty-five years old. (Photo courtesy of Adam Rukawai Wright)

Not really very much to distinguish the front of this coupé from the Series 1 production cars. (Photo courtesy of Adam Rukawai Wright)

Looking towards the boot, things to note are the later S-shaped exhaust pipes and the rear side marker lamps. (Photo courtesy of Adam Rukawai Wright)

This prototype coupé's interior was slightly smaller than that of the production cars. (Photo courtesy of Adam Rukawai Wright)

Breathing New Life into the Project

Lofty England, the erstwhile manager of the Jaguar Cars sports car racing team, who succeeded Sir William Lyons as the company's Chairman and Chief Executive, is credited as being one of the XJ-C's biggest fans. It is thanks to his efforts in 1972 that three more new prototype concept coupés were constructed, ready to be used to add interest to the events that Jaguar planned to attend in 1973. In 1973 itself a further fourteen prototype XJ-Cs would be produced. The announcement that a coupé was joining the XJ line-up was made in 1973, at the same time as the Series 2 was being announced. This was wishful thinking on the part of Jaguar, because the XJ-C would not hit the Jaguar dealers' forecourts until two years later in 1975. In fact, Jaguar developed the XJ-C alongside the XJ-S, and both models were launched in the same year.

In many ways it should have been an easy car to bring into production, as it used many tried and tested components from the XJ saloons. But the delay was largely down to the technical challenges that the coupé posed for Jaguar. The two main problems that Jaguar had to address before the coupé could be launched were the lack of structural rigidity in the coupé's bodyshell, which was a direct result of having the central window pillar removed. They also needed to address issues with excessive wind noise that were caused by the front windows being slightly pulled away from the car's body and their sealing rubbers at high speed.

Jaguar were able to solve the first issue by widening the rear window pillar, which added extra strength to the bodyshell. It was Cyril Crouch, Jaguar's chief body engineer, who is credited with developing the 'Monkey climb' system that was used to operate the XJ-C's rear windows, which helped to make it a pillarless coupé

The second problem was far more complicated. Stephen Ainsworth remembers this problem well, because it happened while he was an apprentice at Jaguar working on the production of the XJ-C and also the XJ-S. The solution that they needed for the coupé's wind noise problem not only had to solve the problem itself, but also needed to be straightforward to implement on the production line.

The closest motorway, the M45, was quiet at night, and regularly used by Jaguar for testing purposes. Stephen recalls the night time sorties, which were part of the effort to eradicate the problem, and often involved high-speed runs in the XJ-C. During these runs he would scrabble around the car's interior trying to identify where the noise was emanating from. The technical solution took a considerable amount of time to develop, and Stephen remembers doing a lot of overtime over the seven-month period while the problem was being worked on. The eventual solution would see a pulley and cable system being employed, which would pull the front windows inwards towards the seals. This worked well and helped to make the coupé almost as quiet at high speeds as its saloon counterpart.

At launch the XJ-C was available in Jaguar form as a 4.2-litre or the 5.3-litre, and for Daimler fans the 4.2-litre Daimler Sovereign and 5.3-litre Daimler Double Six were produced. The American market would get just two options: the XJ6C and the XJ12C. Production figures were fairly modest and would see a total of 10,426 coupés produced during its two-year production run; by the time production ceased on 8 November 1977, these consisted of 6,847 4.2-litre Jaguars and 1,677 4.2-litre Daimlers. The V12 engine cars accounted for 1,855 Jaguars and just 407 Daimler Double Sixes.

Jaguar had always managed to price its cars very competitively compared to other manufacturers, but when it came to the coupé the pricing was more contentious. At £11,755

Outside Eshald House in Yorkshire is this very nice XJ12C. (Photo courtesy of Richard Pierce)

it was over a thousand pounds more than the equivalent XJ12, which, for many, with its four doors, would have been seen as a more practical choice. If Jaguar had continued to produce the coupé alongside the XJ-S, perhaps the extra kudos that it might have gained from competing successfully in the European Touring Car Championships might have paid dividends. But sadly, this was not to be, and both the XJ-C and the Broadspeed XJ-C would experience an untimely demise.

What Might Have Been

Ralph Broad, the Birmingham-based saloon car racer and engineer, already had a good relationship with Leyland in the UK. He was highly thought of as a driver, an engineer, and an expert tuner. In the early days he was part of a thriving tuning and accessory industry that grew up around the BMC's Mini. His company Broadspeed benefitted greatly from his engineering background and his Minis were amongst the best. Perhaps not quite as fast in a straight line as the BMC factory's own Mini Coopers, but they were said to handle better. This would lead to Broadspeed becoming the official works team in 1965 for the BMC Mini Cooper S.

Ralph had identified the racing potential in the V12 XJ-S. But the Leyland executives at the time had other ideas, and put forward the V12 XJ-C as a potential Group 2 contender, for entry into the European Touring Car Championships. Development began in 1975, but this was too late for the 1976 season, and much of this season was missed. When driver

Derek Bell took the Broadspeed XJ-C out for its first outing at the RAC Tourist Trophy at Silverstone in 1976 it performed rather well, lapping the circuit two seconds quicker than BMW's CSL, which was being driven at the time by the then current European Touring Car Champion, Pierre Dieudonné. This incredible performance gave Derek pole position, but sadly his success was short-lived with the coupé's tyres struggling to cope with the car's power, forcing him to reduce his pace and to drop out of contention.

His co-driver, David Hobbs, was also doing well, until a half shaft failure saw a wheel parting company with his car and putting him out of the race. Stephen Ainsworth also recalls that one of the failed Broadspeed hubs was taken to the Radford plant for investigation. Here Jaguar's resident metallurgist, Malcolm Sykes, was able to identify the areas of weakness which had caused the failure. This would lead to the hub strengthening that would stop the failure happening in the future. These changes would also find their way onto production cars, as rules of the competition dictated that the Broadspeed XJ-C must be a version of the production car. This also meant that the Broadspeed XJ-C had some quirky features, such as a walnut dash. In truth the Broadspeed cars were modified, the chassis was acid dipped in an attempt to reduce its weight, and any bracketry or anything else that wasn't required was removed from the car. Stephen also remembers working at Jaguar on producing a lightweight Broadspeed chassis, which, if it had continued into production, would have seen a lightweight Broadspeed car being available to buy for road use, so that it could then enter the European Touring Car Championships.

A lot of problems were caused by the Broadspeed Team not having enough time to fully develop the car off the racetrack, and in actuality they were forced to both develop and race the car at the same time. The Broadspeed XJ-C had a huge amount of potential and continued to show glimpses of what might have been. In 1977 at the Nürburgring circuit driver John Fitzpatrick had achieved pole position after qualifying. He then set a new class lap record from a standing start on the opening lap of the race. But the engines suffered severe problems caused by oil starvation, which led to their ultimate failure. This included John's engine, which would not make the second lap of the race. It wasn't all bad news, because the second XJ-C of Derek Bell and Andy Rouse not only made it to the end of the race, but did so in second place. The solution to this oil starvation problem, which was at least in part caused by the Series 2 sump, was in hand. If the Broadspeed XJ-C had continued racing it would have got a dry sump. To try to get round the problem at the Nürburgring circuit Broadspeed had taken with them twelve wet sump engines.

Just as things looked more promising, Leyland pulled the funding plug in 1977. This was not surprising, as Jaguar had also removed the XJ-C from its range and there was little to gain from having a successful racing Broadspeed XJ-C, as the coupé was no longer a current model. It really wasn't that surprising that Jaguar dropped the XJ-C – sales were not great and they already had the XJ-S, which had been launched in 1975 and was competing for sales with the XJ-C. Some might say that it was surprising that Jaguar had launched the XJ-C at all; however a considerable amount of time and money had been invested in its development and subsequent production over a number of years. As Jaguar were already working on the XJ-C at the end of the 1960s, its conception and production were separated by many years. The original thinking that had prompted Sir William Lyons to want to introduce a pillarless coupé into the XJ range had passed. In 1975 the top-selling cars in the USA were the Oldsmobile Cutlass and the Ford Granada, with not a pillarless coupé in sight.

One of the original Broadspeed XJ12Cs at the Bicester Scramble, October 2021 (car owned by the JDHT).

Another image of the original Broadspeed XJ12C at the Bicester Scramble, October 2021 (car owned by the JDHT).

1978 Jaguar XJ12C Broadspeed in the garage and almost ready for action at the Silverstone Classic 2018 Historic Touring Car Challenge.

1978 Jaguar XJ12C Broadspeed. The British Leyland livery is simple but very effective and looks great. At the Silverstone Classic 2018 Historic Touring Car Challenge.

1978 Jaguar XJC V12 Broadspeed travelling at speed at the Silverstone Classic 2018 Historic Touring Car Challenge.

1978 Jaguar XJC V12 Broadspeed at the Silverstone Classic 2018 Historic Touring Car Challenge. What a shame they were never able to fulfil their racing potential.

Two Notable XJ-Cs

Jaguar's once rather unloved, but now rather popular, XJ-C has succeeded in capturing popular imagination over the years. One example of this is what appears to be a Broadspeed coupé, which was featured in a popular television programme of the seventies, *The New Avengers*. The car that was used in the television programme was a Broadspeed-bodied XJ-C, but it actually had standard XJ running gear. One of the two episodes that it featured in was entitled *The Three Handed Game*, and saw actor Patrick Macnee, who portrayed John Steed, drive the coupé round a racetrack in pursuit of a race driver who was doing practice laps in his racing car. This coupé, which has had a rather chequered existence since this iconic performance, now finds itself at Classic Jaguar for restoration.

Another famous coupé belongs to Harry Metcalfe, creator of the very popular YouTube channel 'Harry's Garage', which has around 600,000 worldwide followers. Harry has had this particular XJ-12C for nine years, but it has recently gone through an extensive and expensive restoration which has been followed on his YouTube channel. The restoration started back in 2021, although it is only fairly recently that some issues with the car's engine seem to have been resolved. The costs involved in the restoration of Harry's coupé are quite eye watering, if unsurprising. The original car was purchased for £5,000 in 2014,

The Avengers Broadspeed XJ when it came up for auction at auction house H&H Classics.

Harry Metcalfe's XJC V12, now in a specially mixed colour which is based on Aston Martin's Minotaur Green.

Harry Metcalfe's XJC V12. The interior of this manual coupé is largely unchanged but does sport a bespoke steering wheel.

Above: Harry Metcalfe's XJC V12. The engine was treated to an extensive rebuild but is still a 5.3-litre unit.

Left: Harry Metcalfe's XJC V12. The fuel injection system proved to be one of the biggest headaches and it took a lot of work to get the coupé running properly.

and then it had another £5,000 worth of upgrades and enhancements, mostly suspension improvements. The latest restoration has seen £34,000 being spent on the bodywork, paint and interior. The V12 engine has been extensively overhauled at a cost of £21,000, but is still a standard 5.3-litre unit, including reusing Harry's enlarged throttle bodies and a newer fuel injection system. This makes the total cost for this car around £67,000.

The last episode in the series of restoration videos was the most interesting because, although the dyno testing clearly showed that the engine was developing just shy of 350 bhp and around 374 lb ft of torque, it was still incredibly civilised and very much a Jaguar. Mated with the manual gearbox, the turbine-like engine has bags of power and just seems to keep giving. I think Harry was properly smitten with his coupé (and who wouldn't be), which is now finally, after a number of false starts, well and truly sorted.

One More Lightweight

Jaguar themselves were working on a lightweight version of the Broadspeed XJ-C, a vision which was never realised. While I was at Tom Barclay Racing recently something caught my eye, tucked away in the far corner of the workshop and covered by a dust sheet. Tom is in the process of creating a lightweight Broadspeed XJ-C for a client in the Far East, who will use it for racing.

The whole process started with a standard coupé bodyshell which now sports a full bespoke roll cage. The front end looks fairly standard, but it can be lifted off in one piece. What looks like a standard bonnet with two wings either side of it is a one-piece front end made of fibreglass, which is incredibly light. Other rather nifty enhancements include a driver's door, which is also made of fibreglass, that simply lifts off to allow the driver easy access to the car's interior.

The construction underneath the bonnet looks similar to that of an E-Type with a frame which extends from the chassis rails, providing the strength and support that is needed. Most of the running gear will be fairly standard XJ. But I know that Tom will be using his own extensive racing experience to produce a driver's car that doesn't disappoint, and is properly set up for racing. It will of course also benefit from whatever engine Tom decides to put in it, potentially a 7.3-litre V12.

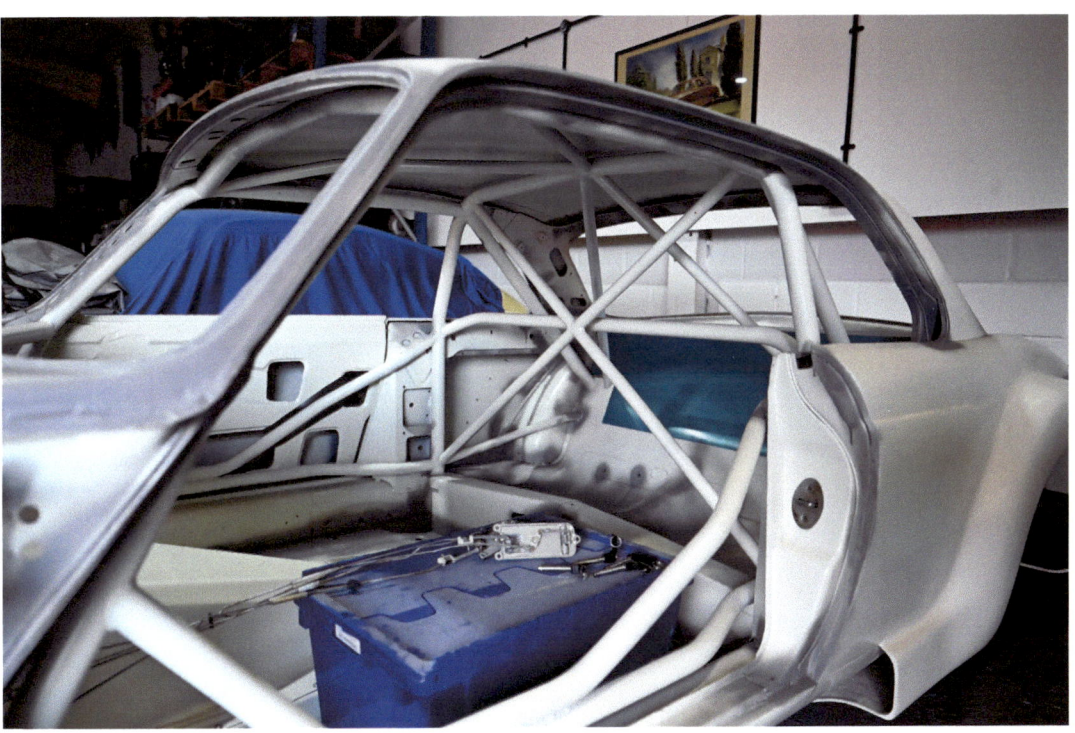

Tom Barclay's lightweight Broadspeed creation. This coupé is fitted with a bespoke roll cage and the driver's door simply lifts off for easy driver access.

Above: The coupé's chassis rails have been extended to become part of the new frame.

Below: It appears that this coupé has a separate bonnet and front wings, but these are a single piece which simply lifts on and off. Being fibreglass, it is incredibly light compared to the original steel panel work.

I'm very much looking forward to seeing Tom finding some time to continue work on this build.

Series 3 XJ: 1978–1992

I always loved cars as a boy and still have my model car collection. I now have fourteen real classic cars, which is too many! I always loved the Series 1 XJ that my local builder had for years in pale blue. I was told the one classic car you must own in your life is an XJ – there's no ride like it. Beats a Rolls-Royce. I was looking for an early XJ but found it difficult to find one in a good unmolested condition so when my Series 3 Daimler XJ VP Sovereign in an unusual gold paint appeared for sale, I had to have it. The rest is history, and I love it.
  Martin Gillingham, owner Series 3 Daimler Sovereign Vanden Plas 4.2-litre auto

The Real Italian Job

In late 1955 HRH Prince Philip paid an official visit to the design office of BMC at their Longbridge plant. While there he was given a sneak preview of the up-and-coming models. His opinion of these planned new models probably was not what the eager executives gathered there for his visit would have wanted to hear. He said that the new models were staid and unadventurous. He suggested that if they wanted to make attractive and appealing cars, they should seek assistance from the Italian design houses. This advice must have been well received, because they commissioned Pininfarina of Turin to design a number of upcoming models. These included the A40, which would later be used as a template for hatchback development. In the medium to larger saloon category, they were responsible for the very popular Austin Cambridge and Morris Oxford designs, which would latterly become known as the Farina saloons. These saloons would dominate their sector of the British car market throughout the 1960s. Other cars that would benefit from the influence of Italian design were Austin Morris' 1100 to 1300 range. BMC were not the only British company to benefit from Italian design; others included Triumph, AC, Aston Martin and Rolls-Royce. One of the most iconic Italian designs must be the 1963 Aston Martin DB5, which was designed by Touring of Milan.

The Series 1 XJ6, the Series 2 XJ6, and the Series 3 XJ12.

The Series 1 Daimler Sovereign, Series 2 Daimler Sovereign and the Series 3 Daimler Vanden Plas.

However, Jaguar had always done their own product development and vehicle design in house, often in a rather chaotic and haphazard way. Things were about to change. In Jaguar's early days, under the strong design leadership of Sir William Lyons, one of the company's strengths had been their ability to design and build great cars (often very quickly, such as the XK120) and offer them for sale at very competitive prices compared to other motor manufacturers. The strength of the product itself had helped Jaguar to make it through some rather dark times, where production standards and virtually non-existent quality control led to poor build quality. Because of the underlying strength of the design, the Series 2 Jaguar had weathered the storm (just about). But this situation had come to a head, and if Jaguar was to survive, things had to change. The XJ had been the mainstay of Jaguar production for over ten years, and a new model was urgently needed to help them to remain competitive and continue to sell well.

Quintessentially, it would have to be every inch a Jaguar, but at the same time the ageing Series 2 XJ needed a facelift. Was it even possible to achieve this; could it be done? A new XJ that continued to offer the best in engineering, style and comfort but which at the same time bought something new to a much-loved design? Initially Jaguar's efforts had concentrated on a direct replacement for the XJ, which would become known as the XJ40. It became clear that this exciting new model simply would never be ready in time to act as a direct replacement for the Series 2. Jaguar had a problem: they needed a new model, but didn't have one. Jaguar's own design team were already over-stretched with the XJ40 project and they just didn't have the spare capacity to work on anything else. The only option that was left for Jaguar was a new one for the company's history: to look for help from outside with the redesign of the XJ. This decision would prove enormously fortuitous for Jaguar. It is highly unlikely, even if they had had the capacity, that they could have come up with the design which many feel was the ultimate development of the XJ Series of saloons.

There is a clear natural progression that can be traced through the XJ saloon range from its inception in 1968 to 1979 when the Series 3 would be launched. Doug Thorpe, who had worked with Sir William Lyons while they were at Jaguar together, would ultimately make the decision which saw Italian design house Pininfarina being engaged to redesign the XJ.

As a design house, Pininfarina designs were in demand not only with British companies, but they also worked closely with Fiat and Ferrari on other iconic designs. The head of Pininfarina, Sergio Pininfarina, had used an XJ12 as the basis for a vehicle that he designed for his own personal transport. This particular design would be offered to Jaguar at a later stage as a possible option for the XJ40. In 1974 Pininfarina were given the contract for the redesign of the Series 2 XJ6 and XJ12. There were limitations; there were to be no changes to the vehicle's underpinnings and the Series 2 floorpan would remain unchanged. The passenger compartment could be changed, and the front and rear of the XJ could also be altered. But it was stipulated that the vehicle's pressings could not be changed. Almost as soon as Pininfarina submitted the first designs for the revised XJ to the British Leyland board, the whole project was put on hold, because of the financial woes of the company as a whole. Things would remain in stasis until 1976, when once again the project would be reinvigorated.

The Series 3, 4.2-litre Vanden Plas. The front quarterlight was deleted and this along with other changes gave the cabin a lighter feel, making it feel more spacious.

The Series 3, 4.2-litre Vanden Plas. The revised front end of the Series 3 still looks fresh today, the lower air intake grille has gone and the front screen has a greater rake than the Series 2.

The Series 3, 4.2-litre Vanden Plas. Pininfarina managed to give the XJ new appeal while keeping the traditional look of the XJ. Sir William Lyons was impressed by this budget refresh.

The Series 3, 4.2-litre Vanden Plas. The Vanden Plas name signified the top-of-the-range qualities of the XJ range, and was the third most expensive XJ at around £17,200. If you wanted a Double Six Vanden Plas this would add a further £3,000 to the price tag. Only the Jaguar XJ12 was more expensive at £21,000.

Jaguar Begins to Regain Independence

Meanwhile, changes instigated by the new Chairman of British Leyland, Michael Edwardes, in November 1977, would see Jaguar and other companies under the British Leyland umbrella start to get their individual identities back. Jaguar were joined together with Triumph and Rover, but despite this they were given more operational independence.

The factory at Castle Bromwich, which was home to the Pressed Steel Fischer body plant, now became part of Jaguar. For the first time in its history, Jaguar had its own dedicated body plant. This had always been something that Sir William Lyons wanted, but he had not had the physical fitness to deliver himself. Sir William's biographers surmised that were it not for the death of his son, he may have been given the task of developing an in-house body production plant for Jaguar. British Leyland had spent £15 million on the paint shop at Castle Bromwich, but the quality of the paintwork produced by this facility was poor. Prior to 1979 Jaguars had been painted at Browns Lane, and when the Jaguar paint shop moved to Castle Bromwich it was not unusual for cars to return to Browns Lane for paintwork rectification. Originally it had been planned to offer a range of seventeen colours to Series 3 XJ owners. Because of the limitations of the Castle Bromwich facility it would not be until much later in 1981 that all these colours could be offered to customers as an option.

Series 3 Project Back on Track

In 1976 work recommenced on the Series 3. A date was set for the launch, which was planned to be at the British Motor Show in October 1978. £7 million were allocated to enable the necessary changes to take place, to enable production to go ahead. At Jaguar the engineering team was led by Bob Knight and Jim Randle, who were based at Browns Lane. The Italian design had delivered exactly what had been asked for; the new XJ was identical to the old one below the swage line. Above the swage line it was completely different. Things like the bumpers, lights and door handles would all change. More subtle but equally important changes included a far more raked windscreen and its associated pillars. The rear screen had been changed, making it almost vertical, and the rear seating compartment was moved back slightly. The front quarterlights (which had been a feature of both the Series 1 and 2 cars) were removed in the new design and this increased the glass area of the car by 7.5 per cent. This was a clever touch because it allowed more light into the car's interior, making it feel larger and more spacious. This small change helped to make the interior feel different, despite it not being altered.

The Series 3 would have flush-fitting door handles and injection-moulded bumpers. There would no longer be separate sidelights and the indicators were housed in the new bumpers. The grille was changed and became crisper and more refined. The lower air intake grille, which is positioned below the front bumper, would lose its grille, helping it to disappear into the background and make it less visible. At the rear of the new XJ, the rear lights were redesigned to fill the space that had previously been occupied by the bumper overriders. Reversing lights would move into these new rear light clusters and the boot would get a new boot plinth.

The three designers at Pininfarina that were responsible for the XJ project, Sergio Pininfarina, Leonardo Fioravanti, and Renlo Carli, had managed to do what to some would have seemed impossible. The new Series 3 design was a triumph, despite being low cost and involving minimal additional tooling for Jaguar. It gave Jaguar a fresh new model. This new model looked different, but at the same time paid homage to the XJs that had preceded it.

The XJ range at launch would include the V12, which was fitted with the Bosch Jetronic fuel injection system. This system would also be used on the 4.2-litre XJ, but the 3.4-litre XJ would remain on twin SU carburettors, two HIF7s. The 3.4-litre car may have remained on carburettors because this was the entry-level model and it would help to differentiate it from the other XJs in the range. Other options would include a five-speed manual transmission, using a gearbox that had originally been developed by Triumph, but that had been further developed by Jaguar. Jaguar engineer Harry Mundy had designed and developed a five-speed manual transmission for Jaguar, which was built at their Radford plant. Using his design these five-speed gearboxes had already been assembled, but they would later be scrapped. We may never know why this Jaguar-designed gearbox failed to make it into production. Perhaps the Triumph gearbox was cheaper to build? The V12-engined cars would be offered with the three-speed GM400 gearbox, which would also be an option that customers could specify on the 4.2-litre XJs.

Jaguar's flagship, the top-of-the-range Series 3 XJ12, with Pepperpot alloy wheels.

The Series 3 XJ12's impressive styling is viewed by many as the pinnacle of the Series 1, 2 and 3 XJs.

The Series 3 XJ would receive a number of other options which were being made available for the first time on any Jaguar. These included cruise control, an intermittent wash wipe function for the windscreen wipers and a headlamp wash wipe system. The seating was altered so that it offered more support and improved comfort for passengers. Electric seats were offered as an option, but they were included as standard on the Vanden Plas models. The instruments, apart from those that were supplied to the USA, were changed from words to symbols.

The Series 3 XJ was still extensively tested despite it using proven engineering. The engineers working on the Series 3's development would make tweaks to the car, further improving the ride and the feel of the car's steering. Norman Dewis, the then test driver for Jaguar Cars, would lead the team that would start testing and clock up many miles in the Series 3 XJ. Testing started in July 1977 at the Motor Industry Research Association (MIRA) and would continue until October that year. The MIRA proving grounds are based at the former Lindley RAF airfield and offer 760 acres of facilities aimed at giving manufacturers testing facilities which offer them the opportunity to fully test a vehicle on a number of different environments and terrains.

Not surprisingly the Series 3 did not make its planned launch date of October 1978. It was, however, launched the following year on 28 March 1979. The base model would feature the 3.4-litre engine on twin HIF7 SUs, and the interior would have cloth upholstery. The entry model-level price was fixed at £12,750. Other models would be offered with cloth upholstery as a no-cost option, but leather would remain the most popular choice with Jaguar's customers.

Thanks to an excellent re-imaging by Pininfarina of the Series 2 XJ, Jaguar now had its new model. Once again, the new Jaguar was well received by the world's motoring press.

But there was still a major hurdle that Jaguar would need to address, and if it couldn't the new XJ, and Jaguar itself, would be stopped in its tracks. Jaguar were in desperate need of a world-class production facility, capable of turning out world-class cars. This was not going to happen overnight and it would need a rather special person to provide the leadership that would help Jaguar to achieve this goal. That person would come in the form of Sir John Egan. He arrived at Jaguar in April 1980, after he accepted an invitation from Sir Michael Edwardes, British Leyland's Chairman, to become Jaguar's new Chief Executive.

Help from a Pair of Safe Hands

Egan was well aware of the challenge that lay ahead, but had seen that Sir Michael had started to get some traction in addressing the endemic problems of the British Leyland Group as a whole. He had also been witness to the demise of other British companies such as Triumph and MG, and was keen that Jaguar should not follow their lead. Not many people have a first day like John Egan – he arrived at the Jaguar factory gate to be greeted by the striking workforce and then had to cross the picket line to get to his new office.

Sir William Lyons and John Egan developed a mutually beneficial relationship which would see Sir William once again become involved with the company he loved, enabling Egan to benefit from his long experience. John Egan and Jaguar designer Doug Thorpe took a Series 3 XJ with them to Wappenbury Hall for Sir William Lyons to examine in detail. Sir William had not lost any of his highly developed design acumen, and was able to point out areas where the new design had clearly succeeded as well as other areas where it had

It is only fitting that the Series 3 XJ12 should have Jaguar's sublime V12 engine. Also note the new rear light clusters, which now incorporate the reversing lights.

Above: Jaguar's flagship, the top-of-the-range Series 3 XJ12. The beating heart of the car.

Below: Although the seats had been redesigned, the Series 3 XJ12's interior has clear similarities to the Series 1 XJ –just a great place to be.

The interior of the Series 3 XJ12 feels and looks very much like a top-of-the-range Jaguar should. Jaguar offered cruise control for the first time.

not. One thing that certainly impressed him had been how the Series 3 XJ refresh had only involved minimal expense for Jaguar. For as we know, Sir William had never liked to waste money or to spend it inappropriately.

Before John Egan joined Jaguar, yearly production figures and resulting worldwide sales were at a low level. In 1979 14,861 Series 3 XJs were sold. Under his supervision, and helped by his quest for improving quality control, worldwide sales would rise to 29,751 by 1983. In May 1987 the last the Series 3 XJ was produced at Browns Lane and went straight into the collection held by the Jaguar Daimler Heritage Trust. (JDHT). This would also be the year that Jaguar would officially launch the XJ40. The Series 3 XJ12 would continue to be produced at the pilot track at Browns Lane in small numbers until 1992. The very last Series 3 to be produced was a Daimler Double Six, which was taken straight to the JDHT. A total of 177,244 Series 3 XJs were produced, making this the most successful of the three iterations of the XJ.

For twenty-four years the XJ Series of saloons had been Jaguar's flagship offering, a real testament to the design that Sir William Lyons started work on in the early 1960s, and the engineers that helped him to build one the best saloon cars the world has ever seen.

At the Heart of Every XJ

A Tale of Two Engines

Every XJ produced at Browns Lane was powered by either a variant of the XK engine or their legendary V12, which was developed from it. In production the XK engine has been available as a 2.4-litre, 2.8-litre, 3.4-litre, 3.8-litre, and 4.2-litre. The 2.4-litre and 3.8-litre XK engines were not used in an XJ, but had a spell in the Mark 1 and Mark 2 compact saloons. The 3.8-litre engine was also used in the E-Type and the Mark X. All these variants had the same basic configuration: a straight six cylinder with DOHC and two valves per cylinder, one inlet and one exhaust. They all had a cast-iron block and an aluminium cylinder head. The 2.8-litre engine was developed specifically for the Series 1 XJ6 in answer to the need to be able to provide an engine of less than 3 litres for corporate customers.

During its development phase the XK engine started out as a 2-litre four-cylinder engine. This engine had the same basic configuration as the XK engines that would follow it; it had two chain-driven overhead camshafts, two valves per cylinder, hemispherical combustion chambers and twin SU carburettors. Working behind the scenes at Jaguar on the development of the XK series of engines were a trio of engineers: William Heynes, Walter Hassan, and Claude Bailey. They carried out the first test run of a six-cylinder XK engine in September 1947. After the first test run it became clear that the six-cylinder power unit was far smoother than its four-cylinder counterpart. Unsurprisingly it was then chosen for further development over the four-cylinder version. It had clear advantages over the four-cylinder unit, and it was also likely that Jaguar could not afford to develop both engine types at the same time.

When it became clear that the Mark VII was not going to be completed in time for the 1948 Earls Court Motor Show, Sir William Lyons, William Heynes and Fred Gardner proved their versatility by coming up with the design for a brand-new two-door sports car in just three days. The XK120 would be powered by the newly designed 3.4-litre XK engine with twin SU carburettors. Initially the XK120 was purely a design exercise with the aim of showcasing Jaguar's latest 3.4-litre XK engine. But as we know the two-door sports car was so well received that it was immediately put into production.

Jaguar's versatile XK engine. Here you can clearly see one of two chain-driven camshafts.

Jaguar's versatile XK engine, which has appeared in production cars as a 2.4-litre, a 2.8-litre, a 3.4-litre, a 3.8-litre, and a 4.2-litre.

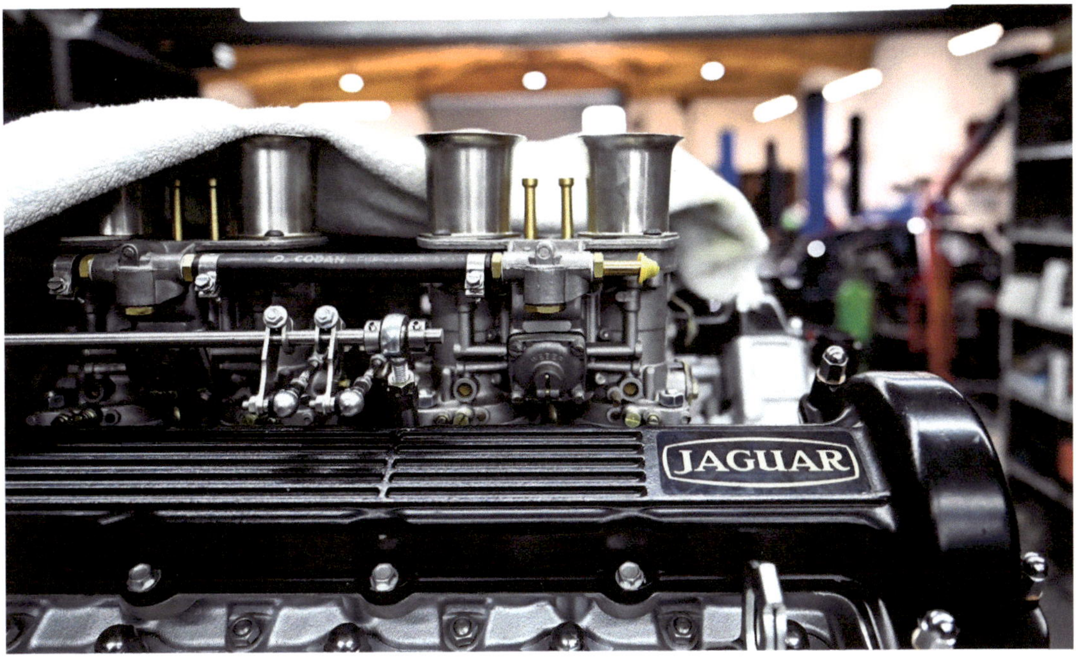

Currently a work in progress but not far off completion: Jaguar's legendary V12 engine.

One very pleasing way to fill an engine bay is with a V12.

In racing, the 3.4-litre engine powered the C type Jaguars, which made their official debut at the Le Mans twenty-four-hour race in 1951. Previously, six cars had been unofficially entered in the 1950 Mille Miglia under the drivers' names (rather than Jaguar's name), and similarly Jaguar entered three cars in the 1950 Le Mans race, also under the drivers' names. Norman Dewis famously took a highly modified XK120, MDU 524, to Jabbeke in Belgium for a speed trail in October 1953, where the 3.4-litre engine propelled the car and Norman to an incredible 172.412 mph for the flying mile.

In 1958 the XK engine was increased in size to 3.8 litres, after which it was used in Jaguar's very successful D types. It was also used in the XK150S and the Mark X saloon. When it was fitted to the E-Type and the Mark X saloon it had triple 2-inch SU carburettors. Seeking a further increase in power, the XK engine was then enlarged to 4.2 litres and would be used in both the E-Type and the 420 and 420G saloons.

It wasn't at all surprising that the trusted and well-tried XK engine was then used for the Series 1 XJ6. It was by this time an old friend that had proved how extremely versatile and reliable it was in a variety of different engine sizes. Originally a V12 engine had been planned for the launch of the XJ, but it wouldn't be until 1971 that a V12 would become a reality, when it became available in the E-Type.

In the process of being built up, the V12 will be ready soon.

With triple SUs, the XK engine in an E-Type.

Tanks for That

Jaguar were keen to capitalise on both their investment in, and the success of, the XK engine, by exploring additional uses for the power plant. After the successful completion of demanding and arduous military testing, the 4.2-litre variant became the engine of choice for the Alvis Scorpion range of light tanks and tracked armoured vehicles. In military use the 4.2-litre XK engine had a single downdraft Solex carburettor, rather than the twin SU carburettors used on production cars. The distributor was waterproofed, as were the HT leads and the engine's breathing system was modified to prevent the possibility of engine fires. The tappets used in military engines were larger, which along with other changes helped to reduce the potential of valve seat wear. A military vehicle needs to be able to operate all over the world where quite often fuel quality would be variable. To help the XK engine cope with these changes in fuel quality its compression ratio was lowered, allowing it to run on lower-octane fuels.

The twin SU fuel pumps found on the XJ Series production cars were replaced by a single military grade fuel pump located on top of the engine. This was a better location for maintenance purposes, but also kept it as far away as possible from any water that might enter the engine compartment. The XK engine was successfully used in the Scorpion, Scimitar, Samaritan and Samson ranges of military vehicles. Eventually it would be superseded by a Cummins diesel engine. There are still a large number of these military engines around; they are quite distinctive and easy to recognise because of the green colour that the engine blocks and cylinder heads were painted. They are still useful, particularly for the parts that they can yield for engine builders and rebuilders.

Although the XK engine is no longer used in any modern Jaguar, it had an amazing lifespan of around seventy years. Very close to 700,000 XK engines of various sizes were built and, as we know, it was the mainstay of the engines that were fitted to and powered the Series 1, Series 2 and Series 3 XJ6 Jaguars and Daimlers. From a production run of 98,527 Series 1 cars, 94,414 had XK engines. For the Series 2, of the production run of 127,961 cars, 107,081 had XK engines. Finally, in the Series 3 production run of 177,244, 122,702 had XK engines. This equates to about 80 per cent of all XJs ever to leave the Browns Lane factory – a considerable achievement. The last production XK engine was installed in a Daimler DS420 limousine in 1992. This Daimler, L420 YAC, is part of the vehicle collection held by the JDHT.

A V12 Engine Finally Makes It into Production

The XJ range of cars were not limited to the six-cylinder XK engines; they were also available with an engine that has to rank amongst one of the finest production V12 engines ever made. This was an engine that was a direct decedent of the XK. As early as 1952 a Jaguar works order existed for experimental project ZX/ZP505, which was to be an XK 4.9-litre V12 engine. This early V12 comprised of two 3.4-litre XK units mounted in a 60-degree V and they shared a single crankshaft. We don't hear much more about the V12 until Walter Hassan returned from Coventry Climax in 1963, where he had been involved in working on engines to power Formula One racing cars. While he had been away development work had continued on a quad cam V12. The JDHT note that he was not impressed with this 5-litre V12 because he believed that it was too large, heavy and complex, and that it would not fit into the XJ. This quad cam engine was also too big to be fitted into the standard E-Type and because it was a complex engine to build, associated production costs would be considerable. Eventually a single overhead cam (SOHC) version of the V12 was installed in a Mark X. This was then tested against a Mark X fitted with the dual overhead camshaft (DOHC) V12. Once again, the value of practical testing was apparent and quickly revealed that the SOHC variant was not only smoother but was more efficient than the DOHC engine, making it the obvious choice for continued development in production cars.

In 1968, while continuing to develop the V12, Jaguar started looking for a fuel injection system for the car. A number of options were considered, and because a suitable system was not available in the UK, an American system became the preferred option. The AE-Brico system was found to work well and became Jaguar's first choice. Unfortunately for Jaguar the company producing this system decided to discontinue its production shortly before Jaguar planned to start V12 production themselves. If this had not been the case the first production XJ12 would have been supplied with electronic fuel injection. Having to look around for a last-minute alternative to this system, Jaguar went for four Zenith Stromberg CDE 175 carburettors.

Another view of Jaguar's much-loved V12 engine.

According to the JDHT, Lofty England commented 'the V12 engine was never supposed to go into the E-Type in the first place, but because the future project, the XJ-S, was a long way off, it got into the E-Type. The E-Type was never designed for the V12, it was good luck that we managed to get it in.' The all-aluminium SOHC V12 engine was produced at a dedicated Jaguar production facility based at Radford. A cast-iron variant had been produced and tested for noise during the engine development phase. As expected, it was considerably heavier than its aluminium counterpart, but after testing it was not found to be any quieter. This was fortunate because the all-aluminium V12 engine is very similar in weight to the 4.2-litre engine, and this would mean that the number of engineering changes required when it was installed in Jaguar's existing XJ would be minimised.

The new engine production facility at Radford was developed by Jaguar at a cost of almost £3 million (at 2023 values that equates to roughly £60 million). This was a considerable investment by Jaguar in their new engine. Fully assembled V12 engines were bench tested at Radford after production before being transported by road to Browns Lane, ready for installation. Less than a year later, in 1972, the V12 became available in the XJ12, which for a time became the fastest production saloon car in the world. In 1973 the original Stromberg carburettors would be replaced by a Bosch D Jetronic fuel injection system.

Tom has a proven racing track record; he still enjoys taking the unwary for a spin, often for charity. This is his coupé.

At the time of the V12's launch, Walter Hassan noted that the engine had a number of further development possibilities. These were later to be realised when an experimental 6.4-litre V12 was tested in the XJ12 prototypes. Development is expensive, and the necessary finance for further development only became available in the 1980s. This saw the 5.3-litre V12's 5,343 cc capacity increase to 5,994 cc and following this the enlarged engine would appear in the highly acclaimed 6-litre XJR-S at the end of the 1980s.

Further development of the V12 would continue in the late 1980s at Tom Walkinshaw Racing, the company that had been founded by touring car racer Tom Walkinshaw in 1976. Under his guidance the V12 would reach what many believe was its full potential. This led to the production of a 7-litre and 7.4-litre V12 engine, which were very successfully used in the XJR-9 and the XJR-12. It is possible to build larger V12 engines, but these would be likely to be more prone to failure, whereas the 7.4-litre V12 is a very robust unit, which is ideally suited for race and road applications.

The last production V12, a 6-litre variant, would roll off the production line in 1997 and would be installed in P60 SOV. Because of the huge success of these two engines, the XK and the V12, Jaguar effectively only had to build two engines during the impressive and lengthy XJ production run. It is easy to underestimate the contribution these two engines made, not only to the XJ range of cars but also to Jaguar as a whole. Proof, if it were needed, that by choosing the right engineers for the job, Sir William Lyons had created an ideal situation which had led to the development of two iconic engines. These engines were the beating heart of Jaguar cars and continue to be an invaluable part of every Series 1, 2 and 3 XJ.

Often seen at hill climbs and other events, Tom's race-prepared Mark 1.

Jaguars and Daimlers at their spiritual home, Wappenbury Hall.

A Sad Goodbye

My journey with Jaguars started in the early '70s with my dad having several Jaguars, but the car that really made a lasting impression as a fourteen-year-old was the 1978 Daimler coupé in squadron blue. Fast forward forty years and I was looking for a project for us to restore together. ARF 530T came up on the internet as a 'barn find', not a coupé but it was in very good condition considering it was laid up for eleven years with 36,000 on the clock. Although being solid it did require some paintwork and new windscreen rubbers, so I decided whilst the windows were out on a full respray. With that decision made it seemed easy to take it to the next level with everything that looked tired being restored or replaced or re-chromed. It's like being fourteen years old again, but I'm in the driving seat now.

Graham Monks, owner Series 2 Daimler Sovereign 4.2-litre auto

Will the Demise of Their Flagship XJ Signal the End for Jaguar?

In February 2021 the short-lived CEO of Jaguar Cars, Thierry Bolloré, made an announcement that would both shock and surprise the motoring world. He took an unprecedented decision and announced that Jaguar, as part of its Reimagine plan, was cancelling the planned XJ. The very XJ whose roots can be traced back to 1968 and before. Having spent around £1.1 billion developing and preparing to bring the car into production, this cannot have been a decision that was taken lightly. The ramifications of this decision would have far-reaching consequences, not only for Jaguar but also for the myriad of companies that would have been part of the new XJ.

Perhaps it was a decision that had failed to understand the role the XJ has played in Jaguar's history? One small crumb of hope was offered to XJ devotees, the news that the XJ name might be revived at some point in the future. This news, however, offered little succour, as it would only probably lead to something that would bear the XJ name, but might not be what is generally understood to be an XJ. This would be very much like the MGs that frequent our highways today, which share very little in common with their humble Abingdon forebears, apart from their octagonal bonnet badges. We have been told that in the future Jaguar will only produce top-of-the-range cars which will be competing with the likes of Aston Martin, Rolls-Royce and Bentley and will sell for around £100,000 each. This at a time when many other manufacturers trade on the success of their high-end cars to sell a range of cars to a wide variety of customers, who buy into the badge but cannot necessarily afford the top-of-the-range offering.

The introduction of the XJ6 in 1968 heralded a time of stability for Jaguar. It streamlined production, replaced a convoluted and puzzling range of Jaguars and Daimlers and created a buzz amongst the car-buying world. Sir William Lyons and his hand-picked engineering team had come up with a world-beating saloon that no other manufacturer could afford to ignore. Demand far outstripped production capabilities, the order books were full, and the new XJ brought prosperity to Jaguar. All this at a price that represented outstanding value for money. Should Jaguar have charged more for the XJ? Certainly, many motoring journalists of the day believed that the new XJ's capabilities far outweighed its price tag. This was just the start of a twenty-four-year period in which the original XJ would be the cornerstone of the Jaguar range. Jaguar's flagship survived the industrial turmoil of the 1970s, the oil crisis, power cuts, and the three-day working week.

Customers continued to buy Jaguars and Daimlers despite poor and at times extremely questionable build quality. It survived the vagaries of American motoring safety legislation, which changed the external appearance of the car, but left its underpinnings largely intact. It weathered the dark days of British Leyland, thanks to the efforts of Sir Michael Edwardes and Sir John Egan. It reinvented itself with the help of Italian design and flair when Pininfarina came up with a design for the Series 3 XJ. Not once, but three times, the XJ saved Jaguar and helped it to prosper. This is because the XJ was, and is, a great car. If you jump into a Series 1 XJ or any XJ today and drive it you will still be impressed by the way it feels and handles. Unlike many of its contemporaries, the excellence of the initial design still shines through; it was right then and it is still right now. The combination of Sir William Lyons' keen eye for design and his engineering team's ability helped him to make his visions a reality.

Until now Jaguar has always appreciated and continued to develop its top-of-the-range offerings on the bedrock which builds on the success of the original range of XJ saloons. The XJ is Jaguar and Jaguar has until now been an inextricable part of the XJ. Without the XJ is Jaguar even Jaguar anymore? Recent announcements of further investment offer some hope, but only time will tell if the Jaguar team can channel the design excellence and market nous of its forebears, and be successful in the creation of a truly reimagined range, one that holds true to the spirit of the company.

Regardless, a small army of Jaguar fans around the world will help to keep the Series 1, 2 and 3 XJ alive, by owning, driving, maintaining, preserving and restoring these fantastic cars.

Bibliography

Books
Clarke, R. M., *Jaguar XJ6 Gold Portfolio 1968-1979* (Cobham: Brooklands Books, 2008)
Egan, John, *Saving Jaguar* (Tenbury Wells: Porter Press International Ltd, June 2015)
Porter, Philip, and Skilleter, Paul, *Sir William Lyons the Official Biography* (Yeovil: Haynes publishing, 2001)
Thorley, Nigel UK, *Jaguar, All the cars* (Yeovil: Haynes publishing, 2003)
Thorley, Nigel, UK, *Original Jaguar XJ* (Bideford: Bay View Books Limited, 1998)

Corporate Literature
75 years Daimler of Coventry: Daimler the first 75 years 1896 to 1971 (Coventry: The Daimler company Limited, 1971)
Jaguar XJ6 Praise Indeed... (Coventry: Jaguar Cars Limited, 1970)
Jaguar XJ6 (sales brochure) (Coventry: Jaguar Cars Limited, 1968)

Magazine Articles
Guiness, Paul, *XJ-C: The last of its kind, Coupé countdown* (Classic Jaguar, October / November 19)
British and Best, Motor Road test, 20/69, Jaguar XJ6 4.2 litre (Motor, May 10 1969)
Patten, Jim, *Coup de coupé* (Jaguar World, April 2000)
Prins, François, *V12: Beast unleashed* (Jaguar Driver magazine, November 2021)
Prins, François, *Powering the future* (Jaguar Driver magazine, April 2021)
Prins, François, *Phoenix Rising* (Jaguar Driver magazine, February 2021)
Seabrook, Ian, *Oldest XJ* (Classic Jaguar, December 18 / January 19)
Waddington, Glen, *The best saloon ever?* (Octane Magazine, Issue 183, September 2018)

Web Resources
Axon, Gary, *10 British cars designed in Italy* (Axon's automotive anorak, May 2022) https://www.goodwood.com/grr/road/news/2022/3/british-cars-designed-in-italy--axons-automotive-anorak/

Bastable, Tony, *Interview with Sir William Lyons* (Drive In, Thames Television, 1977) https://www.youtube.com/watch?v=SZ8oLTEaYnM

Bell, Matt, UK, *Jaguar XJ Series 2 Buyers Guide* (Classics World, Kelsey Media, April 2022) https://classicsworld.co.uk/guides/jaguar-xj-series-2-buying-guide/

Berridge, Declan, *Best of British Cars, Concepts and prototypes: Pininfarina Jaguar proposals* (AROnline, October 2017) https://www.aronline.co.uk/concepts-and-prototypes/pininfarina-jaguar-proposals/#google_vignette

The Best selling cars blog, 1976 https://bestsellingcarsblog.com/1976/01/usa-1975-oldsmobile-cutlass-and-ford-granada-on-top/#:~:text=USA%201975%3A%20Oldsmobile%20Cutlass%20and,top%20%E2%80%93%20Best%20Selling%20Cars%20Blog

Buckley, Martin, *Ralph Broad Obituary* (The Guardian, October 2010) https://www.theguardian.com/sport/2010/oct/21/ralph-broad-obituary

Mayhead, John, *The Jabbeke Speed Trials* (Haggerty Insurance, October 2018) https://www.hagerty.co.uk/articles/the-jabbeke-speed-trials/

MWK 28G, (Website for the world's oldest XJ6) http://mwk28g.co.uk/

Parish, David, *The 1973 – 1975 Energy Crisis and Its Impact on Transport,* (Royal Automobile Club Foundation for Motoring, RAC Foundation, October 2009) https://www.racfoundation.org/wp-content/uploads/energy-crisis-parish-161009-report.pdf

Pininfarina website, *Pininfarina, we move dreams, Heritage collaborations* https://pininfarina.it/en/heritage-collaborations/

Smith, Sam, *Jaguar were right to cancel the XJ, but the rest doesn't make sense* Carscoops March 2001) https://www.carscoops.com/2021/03/opinion-jaguar-were-right-to-cancel-the-xj-but-the-rest-doesnt-make-sense/

Top Gear Episode 1, (BBC, April 1977) https://www.bbc.com/historyofthebbc/anniversaries/april/top-gear/#:~:text=Top%20Gear%20started%20in%20the,pedestrians%20as%20much%20as%20motorists.

Jaguar Daimler Heritage Trust Resources

Joyce Martin, Merrygold Tony, and Prins François, *AJV8 Engine 1996 – Present* https://www.jaguarheritage.com/jaguar-engineering/ajv8-engine/#:~:text=The%20first%20production%20V8%20from,in%20the%20XJ8%20in%201997

Prins, François and Merrygold, Tony, *V12 engine 1971-1977* https://www.jaguarheritage.com/jaguar-engineering/v12-engine/

Prins, François, *Six Cylinder XK Engine 1948-1992* https://www.jaguarheritage.com/jaguar-engineering/6-cylinder-xk-engine/

Prins, François, *Military XK Engine* https://www.jaguarheritage.com/jaguar-engineering/military-xk-engine/

Prins, François, *Walter 'Wally' Hassan Chief Experimental Engineer and Engine Designer* https://www.jaguarheritage.com/jaguar-people/walter-hassan/

Prins, François, UK, *Jaguar C-Type The Race for Le Mans* https://www.jaguarheritage.com/jaguar-engineering/jaguar-c-type-the-race-for-le-mans/

Elpitiya, Shihanki and Merrygold, Tony, *Harry Mundy Ex-Technical Editor of 'The Autocar' and Engine Designer who worked on XK, V12 and AJ6 Engines* https://www.jaguarheritage.com/jaguar-people/harry-mundy/

RACING JAGUARS – Broadspeed XJC V12 https://www.jaguarheritage.com/octane-2014-april-broadspeed-xjc/

1976 Broadspeed XJ12 Coupé https://www.jaguarheritage.com/car/1976-broadspeed-xj12-coupe/

1993 Daimler Double-Six The Last Series 3 Daimler Double-Six Built K530 DDU https://www.jaguarheritage.com/car/1993-daimler-double-six-series-3-saloon/

1987 Jaguar Sovereign Last Series 3 4.2 Litre XJ6 Built D402 GHP https://www.jaguarheritage.com/car/1987-jaguar-sovereign-series-3-4-2-litre-d402-ghp/

Acknowledgements

First of all, a special thank you to Mrs Suth, my copy editor and partner in crime for the last thirty-two years. Most of all for putting up with me when I just had to tell someone what I had just discovered about Sir William Lyons or Jaguar in general. She has told me more than once that she now knows far more about the Jaguar XJ Series 1, 2 and 3 saloons than she ever wanted.

Fred R. Barnard, an advertising executive, once said that a picture is worth a thousand words. I agree wholeheartedly with that sentiment; and thanks to Noel the photos in this book deliver exactly that. Noel, of Noel Skeats Photography, has been with me from the start, since the day we both spotted the coach from the Italian Job parked at the roadside, while on separate journeys to our first meeting. This book would just not be the same without your attention to detail and your fabulous photos.

When you ask someone to do something for you, and they give you just what you were after without any help or guidance, you have to wonder if they are telepathic or perhaps just very good at what they do. And Quentin Willson is certainly very good at what he does. Thank you, Quentin.

A big thank you to Scott Shearman for having the good sense to preserve Sir William Lyons' former home, Wappenbury Hall, for future generations. He allowed us to join him there for our first photoshoot, brought out two fine Jaguars from his own collection, and regaled us with his humorous stories of past Jaguar endeavours. The Wappenbury crew came from near and far to share their passion for Jaguars and to join in with the fun. They were Julian Collis, Simon Currell, Martin Gillingham Graham Monks, Stuart McEvoy and Paul Muncey.

Tom Barclay and Nia took time out of a very busy schedule during the racing season to make us feel welcome at Tom Barclay Racing Ltd, where amongst other things we talked of Jaguar engines and lightweight coupé builds for half a day.

Adrian Massey was kind enough to bring along the world's oldest XJ6, MWK 28G, to my favourite pub on what turned out to be the perfect summer's day. I can tell you that his visit certainly attracted a lot of local interest. As MWK's owner and custodian Adrian has been doing an excellent job of helping others to celebrate the unique history of this very special XJ6 for a number of years.

Thanks are also due to Mats Johansson, who I started chatting with about Tudor Webasto sunroofs quite a few years ago, and who has now become a best friend. He unwittingly provided many of the source documents that I turned to when researching for this book.

I have enjoyed chatting with Adam Rukawai Wright in Australia about his unique pre-production Series 1 XJ-C. Adam is a huge Jaguar fan and just the right person to look after the Jaguar prototype that was initially sent to be scrapped by Jaguar.

Stephen Ainsworth was lucky enough to work as an apprentice at Jaguar when the Series 1 XJ and XJ-C were being developed. It's clearly a time that he enjoyed and his insights and personal experience were both interesting and useful.

The United States of America was a major export destination for Jaguar cars and Sir William Lyons followed developments in the American automotive industry closely. Scott Docie, whose Jaguar journey started in a Daimler Sovereign, helps us get an American flavour with his Californian XJ6C and Series 2 XJ12 saloon.

My thanks are also due to my German shepherd Bailey, who has at times felt that the attention that I have paid to my laptop rather than throwing his Kong has been rather tiresome. And finally, my thanks to the army of Jaguar fans around the world who share their passion for these wonderful cars.

The author and publisher would like to thank the following people/organisations for permission to use copyright material in this book:

For the Jonathon Haynes quote which appeared in Kelsey Media's *Octane* magazine article, 'The best saloon ever?' by Glen Waddington, September 2018

For the Lofty England quote which appears on the JDHT's web site on the web page https://www.jaguarheritage.com/jaguar-engineering/v12-engine/

For the *Daily Telegraph* quote which was written by Dave Selby in the Motoring section of *The Telegraph, Telegraph Motoring*, on Saturday 17 April 2004

For the Jim Tosen quote which appeared in the Jaguar booklet, *Jaguar XJ6 Praise Indeed...* but originally appeared in his *Motor* review of the XJ6 on 21 March 1970

For the production figures quote which appeared in *Sir William Lyons The Official Biography* by Philip Porter and Paul Skilleter, Haynes Publishing 2001.

Every attempt has been made to seek permission for copyright material used in this book. However, if we have inadvertently used copyright material without permission/acknowledgement we apologise and we will make the necessary correction at the first opportunity.

The author with his Daimler enjoying a birthday trip to his favourite wine area of France, the Côtes du Rhône Villages.